Beyond the Basics of Reengineering:

Survival Tactics for the '90s

Beyond the Basics of Reengineering:
Survival Tactics for the '90s

Quality Resources/The Kraus Organization
White Plains, New York, U.S.A.

Industrial Engineering and Management Press
Institute of Industrial Engineers
Norcross, Georgia, U.S.A.

99 98 97 96 95 94   6 5 4 3 2 1

Library of Congress Cataloging-in-Publication Data

Beyond the basics of reengineering : survival tactics for the '90s.
       p.   cm.
  Includes bibliographical references and index.
  ISBN 0-89806-138-5
  1. Production planning. 2. Eastman Kodak Company.
3. Organizational change—Case studies. 4. Production planning—Case studies.
TS176.B489   1994
658.4'063—dc20   94-11395
                                                        CIP

Publisher: Ellen Snodgrass
Editors: Maura Reeves and Eric Torrey
Assistant Editor: Sonja Lee
Cover Design: Susan McBride

ISBN 0-89806-138-5 Industrial Engineering and Management Press
ISBN 0-527-76257-1 Quality Resources

Additional copies may be obtained by contacting either of the following co-publishers. Quantity discounts are available.

Institute of Industrial Engineers
Customer Service
25 Technology Park/Atlanta
Norcross, Georgia 30092 USA
(404) 449-0460 phone
(404) 263-8532 fax

Quality Resources
A Division of the Kraus Organization Ltd.
One Water Street
White Plains, NY 10601
(914) 761-9600
(800) 247-8519

Contents

Part One. Reengineering Methodology and Case Study

Part Two. Case Studies In Development and Implementation of BPR

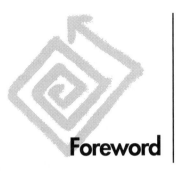

Foreword

If you are like most business people, you are wondering how to help your company compete in today's business environment and how to help position it for survival in the future. The decade of self-help books has transitioned to the decade of company-help books.

Companies are impatiently looking for ways to take giant steps forward, and many companies in the US. have embraced Business Process Reengineering (BPR) as a way to take those steps. In a recent Grant Thornton survey of American manufacturers, 95% of mid-sized manufacturers claim to have reengineered at least part of their company, and 30% say they have reengineered their entire company within the last three years.

You may have heard or read about BPR, but are still uncertain about what it is. Is it just another management technique that will disappear just about the time you've begun to understand it? Does it mean reengineering a department, or a division, or a whole company?

There are a number of books already available that can explain BPR; however, most of the books demonstrate a single methodology/approach to BPR, when in fact, BPR is an evolving business strategy, and there is no one, single methodology. Every company involved in BPR will adapt the process to reflect their particular needs and corporate culture.

To clarify, we begin this book with a detailed, step-by-step case study that followed a very specific methodology. However, we also present ten other case studies that, while having common elements, follow their own paths to achieving the dramatic and radical changes that characterize business process reengineering.

We chose to present the Eastman Kodak Company reengineering methodology as the foundation for this book, because it is based on the teachings and writings of Dr. Michael Hammer, and the supporting methodology developed by Texas Instruments Inc. Examples from Kodak's own reengineering project, Customer Interface and Order Management in the Large Commercial Graphics Market, are intertwined in the methodology chapters. The other case studies were selected to present a mix of companies in manufacturing and service industries. Reading the complete collection brings home the point that no matter what type of organization you work for, the key elements are always the same as you move from one stage of BPR to another.

The companies featured in this book are at various stages in BPR projects. If you refer to the Kodak Reengineering Methodology Framework At A Glance chart on page 14, which details the various common stages in a BPR project, you will see: 1) project initiation, 2) process understanding, 3) new process design, 4) business transition, and 5) change management.

At the time of this publication, some of these companies were in the initiation and understanding stages, some had moved on to new process design and some had reached the business transition stage. Change management is pervasive throughout all of the case studies.

Of special note, two companies, Corning Asahi Video Products Company (CAV), and Eastman Chemical Company received the added boost of awards which, in a way, validated their projects. CAV received the 1993 Corning Quality Award, which was voted on by all Corning employees, beating out 100 nominees. Eastman Chemical Company received the prestigious Malcolm Baldrige National Quality Award.

Some of the companies in this book used internal consultants, from expanding industrial engineering department duties, to developing teams from scratch, to expanding the project team to a center for excellence. Some companies used a combination of internal and outside consultants, from management consultants to universities. All agree, however, that in the final analysis, the process must be internalized in order for the employees to take ownership.

Most BPR projects include some aspect of information systems and this will be evident in several of the case studies. The growth in technology and its ability to network large operations and enable

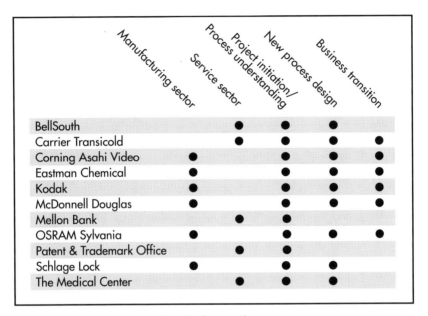

	Manufacturing sector	Service sector	Process understanding	Project initiation/ New process design	Business transition
BellSouth		●	●	●	
Carrier Transicold		●	●	●	●
Corning Asahi Video	●		●	●	●
Eastman Chemical	●		●	●	●
Kodak	●		●	●	●
McDonnell Douglas	●		●	●	●
Mellon Bank		●	●		
OSRAM Sylvania	●		●	●	●
Patent & Trademark Office		●	●		
Schlage Lock	●		●	●	
The Medical Center		●	●	●	

Case Studies at a Glance

faster, simpler communication does provide one element of change in business processes. However, while information systems may be a facilitator in reengineering, it is not the driving force.

No matter what the projects were called, who was on the teams, or which criteria were used, each project reflects a need to meet increasing customer expectations. Customers – both external and internal – were at the forefront of these projects.

We hope that by reading first the methodology, and how Kodak applied it, as well as the case studies at various levels of "completion" you will be able to understand the processes these companies are going through (or have gone through) and see the lessons learned – both positive and negative. We believe that you will be impressed by the candor of those interviewed.

Is BPR just a fad? Is it just turbo-charged TQM? Whatever you may call it, it has the ear of American business right now and will for the next few years of the current economic cycle. Businesses must make fundamental changes in order to survive.

We are pleased to be able to make a contribution to your education and wish you success.

Ellen Snodgrass
Publisher

Acknowledgments

You may occasionally hear someone comment (after completing a written work of some kind) how something was so easy it literally "wrote itself." Well, this book did not write itself — numerous people were involved in the creation of this work — and this is the space where we get to thank all of those involved. Very few people actually read acknowledgments unless, of course, they think they may be one of those folks being mentioned. So, if you are about to leave us here and skip to the next section, know that this book would not be possible if not for the collaborative efforts of the people listed in the next few paragraphs. What that means is — if you read this book, and you like it, please come back and read the acknowledgments and mentally thank these people for all of their efforts.

Maura Reeves and Eric Torrey deserve special thanks for all of the work they put in as editors of this publication. The numerous hours they spent developing/finding stories and writers, editing manuscripts, and producing a book that is both educational and enjoyable to read are evident in the quality of the product you now hold in your hands. Thanks also to Cindy Tokumitsu, of Quality Resources, for reviewing manuscripts, offering suggestions and enthusiastically supporting this project at every step.

The writers of *Beyond the Basics of Reengineering* deserve to be recognized and thanked. David Lester, John Powers and Ralph Harding, all members of the Kodak Reengineering Center for Excellence, collaborated to write Part One of this book. Their willingness to share the expertise they have garnered while working at Kodak was what moved this book beyond the concept stage.

Part Two of this publication was written by four excellent freelance writers who worked hard to learn all they possibly could about BPR before they began interviewing and writing their case studies. Every company that was approached to be included in this book was assured that the writer would be professional, quick and unobtrusive — and not one company was disappointed. As a matter of fact, several companies called the editors to congratulate them on their choice of writers. Thanks to Brad Bambarger, Connie Brittain, John McCloud and Susan Taylor. Thanks also to Susan McBride, the artist who created our cover. Susan had to take our vague ideas of what we thought we might want and solidify them into something real. We are more than pleased with the result of her efforts.

In addition to all of the people who took time from their busy schedules to be interviewed by our writers, we would like to thank the point person(s) at each company who was particularly helpful in getting each case study written with as little difficulty as possible. David Braunstein, director of process improvement at McDonnell Douglas is listed first since he was our first interview. Thank you David for being our test case, for being helpful every time we called back for just one more piece of information, and for waiting patiently for the book to be published while we completed all of the other case studies. Thanks to Sheryl Pounds, and industrial engineer at Schlage Lock Co., who made our job a bit easier by contacting us. Sheryl knew that Schlage Lock had a story to tell before she knew we were working on a BPR book.

Bob Savell at Eastman Chemical is to be commended for arranging and giving successful interviews the week before the Malcolm Baldrige examiners were scheduled to arrive. Congratulations, by the way, on winning one of only two 1993 Malcolm Baldrige National Quality Awards.

Patricia Kelly Lee, reengineering project leader at The Medical Center, was one of our most enthusiastic supporters. She not only arranged interviews at The Medical Center in Pittsburgh, but she also managed — while attending a conference in Chicago — to meet with one of our writers to give a complete background on the BPR project she was involved with.

Thank you Kevin Watts, P.E., director/productivity and quality department at OSRAM Sylvania. Kevin investigated to make sure there was a real story to tell at OSRAM, convinced his colleagues to participate, and did a wonderful job of working with our writer.

Pam Arledge, corporate media manager at BellSouth, was particularly helpful in getting information together for us. You would think since BellSouth is located in the same city as the publishing company producing this book that this case study would have been a breeze. It wasn't. Thank you Pam for putting-up with all of the calls, faxes and courier packages.

The Carrier Transicold case study would not exist if Tom Greenwood, assistant professor at the University of Tennessee, had not called to let the editors know of the exciting things that were happening at that company. Tom was also extremely helpful in arranging interviews and getting the completed manuscript moving throughout the review process — not an easy task considering several of the principals involved were located overseas.

Thanks also to Lorin Brigden, Andersen Consulting, and Marty Deise, MTA/Price Waterhouse. Both of these people tried so hard to find a client that was doing reengineering and would agree to be interviewed by us. After more dead ends than we are sure either of them would like to remember, Lorin arranged for our interview with Corning Asahi Video Products and Marty managed to arrange our interview with the U.S. Dept. Of Commerce/Patent and Trademark Office.

And a special thanks to Margaret Kirch Cohen, APR, manager/media relations at Mellon Bank. Margaret got the dubious honor of working with us on one of the final case studies written for the book with deadlines always looming overhead. Thank you for your help, patience and understanding.

And finally, thank you Dr. Michael Hammer for introducing business process reengineering to all of us.

Part One

Reengineering Methodology and Case Study

By Dave Lester

Overview of Kodak
Reengineering Methodology

Even before business process reengineering (BPR) was described by
Dr. Michael Hammer in his article "Reengineering Work: Don't
Automate, Obliterate" (1990), Eastman Kodak Company was achieving significant improvements in cost, cycle time and quality. However,
the improvements were simply not dramatic enough to meet increasing customer expectations in some important areas. Even when they
were, replicating the dramatic improvements in other areas proved
elusive. Therefore, an approach was needed to bring about these
dramatic improvements in a systematic, repeatable manner. The
approach selected by Kodak is based on the teachings and writings of
Dr. Michael Hammer, and the supporting methodology, developed
by Texas Instruments Inc.

Many of the concepts are best understood through example.
Therefore to aid the learning process deliverables from a Kodak
reengineering project called Customer Interface and Order Management in the Large Commercial Graphics Market (CI&OM LCGM)
are cited. This particular project was selected because it was the first
to use the formal reengineering methodology. The project was
initiated in the Fall of 1992. At the time of this writing the team is
engaging customers in the detailed design of the business processes.
Simultaneously, the information systems are being planned, initial
job applicants are being considered and training is taking place. The
team has committed to these delivering these results:

- Completing customer orders — 55% reduction in steps and 67% reduction in cycle time
- Establishing customer contracts — 93% reduction in cycle time
- Number of documents — 80% reduction
- Number of invoices per order — 80% reduction
- Rework — 80% reduction
- Internal information systems — consolidation
- Electronic orders — 200% increase
- Orders completed in a single call — 300% increase.

What is business process reengineering?

Business process reengineering is about major step level improvement, it is not about incremental improvement. In their book, *Reengineering the Corporation: A Manifesto for Business Revolution,* Hammer and Champy (1993) define reengineering as: "The *fundamental* rethinking and *radical* redesign of business *processes* to achieve *dramatic* improvements in critical, contemporary measures of performance, such as cost, quality, service, and speed." Consider the four key words in this definition.

Fundamental—Reengineering requires introspection. A business must answer the most fundamental of questions. Why do we do what we do? And, why do we do it the way we do it? Asking these questions uncovers the assumptions that underlie the way business is conducted. Those assumptions can be faulty or out of date. When the CI&OM LCGM team asked themselves the second question they realized the way they did things assumed that customers were willing to call back two or three times to complete and confirm an order. In testing that assumption they found that customers felt strongly that one call was the limit.

Radical— Reengineering is about reinventing the business, not enhancing or improving. It requires getting at the root of things and redesigning at that level. It is not about tinkering with what exists in hopes of fixing the existing problem. Solutions that do not go to the root of the problem will be short lived at best, and detrimental at worst. Getting at the root of the problem is possible by looking at the work itself. Too often business has looked at organization structure and/or people as the problem and the cure. "If only we were organized differently X (substitute X with your problem) would go away." Or, "If we only had people with more/different/better skills, or they were better motivated problem X would be solved." Sound familiar? The problem with this approach is it does not get at the root of the problem. Nor is a new organization structure or more training likely to bring about a truly radical and enduring solution.

Dramatic — Reengineering is about making major improvements not about incremental change. The CI&OM LCGM team is redesigning to deliver improvements ranging from 50% to 300%. That's what reengineering must be about. Reengineering is not about getting 5-10% better. If that is your need, use your continuous improvement methodology. The reengineering methodology requires too much effort and pain to be applied for such small gains.

Processes — For many, this is the most difficult concept in reengineering. How many of you, in reading the definition, skimmed right over the word processes? The reason may be that it is perceived as unimportant, or that it is already well understood. But is it? To ensure common understanding it is useful to start with a definition. A business process is a set of activities that takes an input, and creates an output of value to a customer. That is simple enough, but most modern companies organize and manage work around tasks, or areas of expertise not around processes that deliver customer value. Inevitably, this leads to many steps and hand-offs, which introduces the chance for errors and slows the delivery of the value added product or service to the customer. For example, the customer interface and order management process starts with a customer order and matches those orders with other data from inventory and product availability. Customer value is added by suggesting products to meet the customer's need, providing a delivery date, arranging delivery and establishing a payment schedule. Currently, responsibility for these activities are spread across multiple organizations. Reengineering seeks to reduce or eliminate these hand-offs, and the resulting errors, long cycle time and customer frustration that result from being shuffled from one person to the next.

If your business requires change that is fundamental, radical and dramatic, reengineering is the approach that will get you there. The decision to reengineer can be made by examining the gaps between what must be and what is today. As an example, the gaps identified by the CI&OM LCGM team and supported by the sponsor are shown in figure 1, stated in terms of project objectives.

---

1. Customer requirements must be processed completely with a single contact.
2. Customers will have immediate access to product and service information.
3. Sales representatives will be able to spend their time growing the business, rather than resolving CI&OM issues.

Figure 1. CI&OM LCGM: Project Objectives

In order to accomplish these objectives, fundamental, radical and dramatic changes in the business processes, organizational structure, job definitions, performance appraisal, reward systems, and enabling technology would all be required. Virtually every aspect of the existing business! Realizing that this gap was much too large to be closed through traditional continuous improvement techniques the leadership of the LCGM business decided to take a risk by employing the reengineering approach.

As a final point of clarification of what reengineering is, it is useful to be clear about what it is not. Those with a cursory awareness of reengineering might confuse it with some other business improvement activities. However, reengineering is not:

- corporate downsizing;
- automating existing processes;
- implementing a new information system;
- reorganizing or flattening the organizational structure; or
- reducing bureaucracy.

It is quite likely that many of these things will be outcomes of reengineering business processes, but they are not the primary objectives.

Clearly then, reengineering is not the same as continuous improvement (CI). Neither, should it be in conflict with CI. The most fundamental difference is the way one looks at the current state. CI starts with the assumption that the basic structures and processes are sound and improvements can be made within the existing boundaries. Reengineering starts with the assumption that the existing structures and processes are broken and the boundaries must be obliterated. The CI assumption implies starting with what is, understanding the flaws and fixing them while preserving the supporting processes and structures. The reengineering assumption implies understanding what customers require and designing a business system starting with a clean sheet of paper.

Framework of Kodak Methodology

In 1992 Kodak had a number of reengineering projects underway throughout the corporation. Each project used a different consultant and as such a different methodology. Although, some of the projects were quite successful the results were inconsistent and unrepeatable. Worse, it was difficult to apply lessons learned from one project to the next. The people involved were also coming to the realization that understanding reengineering from an academic or theoretical viewpoint was one thing, implementing it was something else altogether. To address these issues, a small team was formed to deliver a methodology for use across the company. The team was allotted eight weeks to complete the task. Given the short time frame it was virtually impossible to develop the methodology from scratch, as Kodak would have been prone to do under similar circumstances in the past. Instead, purchasing an existing methodology appeared to be the most viable solution. That meant establishing selection criteria on which to base the purchase decision. The first step in establishing the purchase criteria was to interview people within Kodak that were involved in reengineering, and to learn from them what they felt were the important features of a methodology. Next the team took advantage of existing contacts at peer firms to learn what methodology they were using, and more important, what they had learned about it through application. Thirdly, the team attended the Michael Hammer seminar, "Reengineering: The Implementation Perspective." At the time Hammer was emerging as the leading thinker and teacher on the subject of business process reengineering, and incorporating his viewpoint was critical to the credibility of the effort.

   That Hammer session led the team to the first of three criteria that was used to evaluate each methodology. That criteria stated: *the methodology must be based on the reengineering concepts of Dr. Michael Hammer.* Insiders and peers involved in reengineering work helped establish the second criteria: *the methodology must be adaptable to a wide variety of situations.* It must handle manufacturing related processes as well as back office business processes. It must be applicable in phases so that projects already underway could take advantage of it. The third criteria was cost oriented. Kodak management insisted that the company not be dependent on high priced external consultants. Therefore, in order to develop internal competence in the reengineering process most of the consulting work would need to be done by Kodak people. The third criteria stated: *the provider must make the methodology available independent of consulting services.*

Of the peer companies and consulting firms contacted, Texas Instruments stood apart in its ability to meet the three criteria, making the choice rather simple. In addition, Texas Instruments was willing to work with the Kodak methodology development team to adapt their methodology to the Kodak environment, to learn how to apply it and to support the methodology long term.

After working with the methodology for over a year, Kodak has achieved the benefits it hoped to attain by buying rather than inventing. Those hoped for benefits were to:

- reduce the risk of project failure by using a proven methodology;
- minimize development, training and project start-up costs;
- minimize the costs of external consultants;
- provide earlier project benefits by starting projects quickly; and
- establish a relationship for regular methodology upgrades.

A couple of points about what to expect of the methodology before describing it in some detail. First, don't expect to see any totally new techniques. The power of the reengineering methodology is not in the application of some new "silver bullet" but in the way it brings proven techniques together, often in a new way, and always with a bolder purpose. Second, while the framework is presented sequentially, it is applied in an iterative manner. Therefore, it is most efficient and ultimately produces higher quality results to move briskly through each step, realizing that future information and insight will enable the team to upgrade the work that has preceded.

Implementation models
The reengineering methodology is based on two models; the Holistic Wheel and the Framework at a Glance. By keeping both of these models in front of the BPR team, and referring to them often the probability of success is greatly improved.

The Holistic Wheel (figure 2) is based on Michael Hammer's "Business System Diamond." In his diamond Hammer depicts four elements that make up a complete business system; business processes, jobs and organizational structure, management systems and beliefs and behaviors. He uses this diamond to describe how and why changes in an organization occur (Hammer, Champy 1993). Texas Instruments adapted Hammer's "Business System Diamond" and upgraded it by adding a circle and three keywords: customers, culture and technology. Understanding the holistic wheel is akin to understanding reengineering, and is a foundation for implementing reengineering. In addition the holistic wheel applies throughout the reengineering effort.

At this point it is appropriate to understand each element of the holistic wheel. The application of the concepts and techniques associated with each element will be developed in the ensuing chapters.

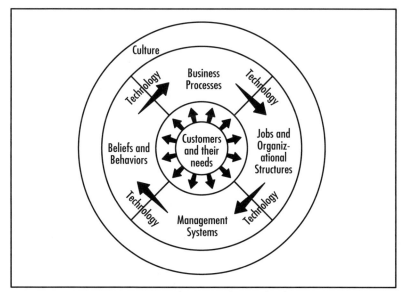

Figure 2. The BPR Holistic Wheel

To understand the holistic wheel, start in the center with the customer. There are two important ideas with respect to the customer. One, the customer must become the center of everything the business does. And, two, customers drive the entire business system. Business processes, organizational structure, jobs, management systems, beliefs and behaviors all must align to deliver on customer requirements. The more a BPR team keeps the customer at the center of their work the more successful it is likely to be.

As was stated previously, a business process is a set of activities that takes inputs, adds value and produces results of value for customers. Even with that seemingly straightforward definition recognizing your business processes may be less than obvious because they are probably unnamed and are not owned by any single organization or manager. Customer interface and order management (CI&OM) is an example of an important business process at Kodak. CI&OM is a customer and process oriented description of Kodak's existing Customer Service, Marketing, Technical Customer Support and Credit organizations. It brings those functional organizations together in a way that makes sense from a customer's point of view.

Redesigned business processes often require redesigned jobs and supporting organizational structure. Often this is the case because jobs and organizations have become more and more specialized as the complexity of the work has increased over time. This specialization has led to organizational inbreeding and isolation. Some of the common symptoms include; frequent 'dotted line' reporting relationships, functional oriented measures and rewards, internal turf battles and many hand-offs required to complete a customer transaction. Traditionally, these problems have been addressed through reorganizing, which in most cases does nothing more than trade one set of problems for another. These reorganizations may result in new relationships but rarely do they affect the work itself: the process. Reengineering requires that the content of the jobs be aligned with business processes, resulting in fewer hand-offs, stronger customer orientation and in most cases more satisfied workers. The example in figure 3 from the CI&OM LCGM project suggests how dramatic these job changes can be.

HISTORICAL	REENGINEERED
Narrow job definitions	Multi-dimensional jobs
Task orientation	Customer orientation
Unclear line of sight to customer	Clear line of sight to customer
Repetitive and routine	Challenging and intense
Many rules and constraints	Broad guidelines with flexibility
Supervisors	Coaches
Managers	Leaders
Command and control	Empowerment

Figure 3. The Nature of Reengineered Jobs

The associated organizational structures, which in this context might include functional support areas, strategic business units, product lines, organization hierarchies, must also be realigned to optimize performance from a customer perspective. Often this means the creation of a multifunctional, team oriented structure with minimal hierarchy.

Management systems establish, reinforce and perpetuate the beliefs and behaviors of employees. Two highly visible processes included in this definition are: budgeting and resource allocation and evaluation and compensation. These management systems must be redesigned to align and reinforce the behaviors required to sustain the new business process. If, for instance, the new business process requires team work, then the evaluation and compensation systems must reinforce team performance over individual performance. If the existing systems don't do that they must be discarded and designed anew. These changes in evaluation and compensation systems are especially important as a wake up call to the enterprise that reengineering is serious, and is out to create radical and enduring change. Figure 4 compares the reengineered compensation concepts being applied by the CI&OM LCGM project team, to their historical approach.

HISTORICAL	REENGINEERED
Individual performance	Team performance
Compensation based on number of people managed	Compensation based on contribution to satisfying customers
Performance appraisal by supervisor	Performance appraisal by team

Figure 4. The Nature of Reengineered Evaluation and Compensation

Continuing clockwise around the wheel leads to beliefs and behaviors. Beliefs and behaviors are intertwined in that beliefs are formed over time as people observe the behaviors that are recognized and reinforced by management and peers. Once formed, these fundamental beliefs drive future behavior, thus becoming self perpetuating. Aligning the beliefs and behaviors of an organization to support the new business process is critical to successful implementation. It can be also easier said than done. One successful approach to changing behaviors and eventually beliefs is through a systematic, data-oriented approach to managing people. This approach known as performance management follows a proven theory of human behavior. That is, given the appropriate antecedents, clear expectations, for example and well understood consequences, such as personally desirable reinforcement, that appropriate behavior can be learned and repeated. Performance management requires consistency and repetitiveness on the part of all involved. One slip into the old mode can undo weeks of progress. Frequent slips can destroy credibility, causing people to retrench and slow the transition to the reengineered environment (Daniels, Rosen 1983). Figure 5 depicts the changing beliefs in the CI&OM LCGM environment.

HISTORICAL	REENGINEERED
My boss pays my salary	Team performance
My work does not matter	I make a real difference
Financial focus	Operational focus
Look out for #1	We're in this together
Succeed by empire building	Succeed by performing
Tomorrow will be like today	No one knows about tomorrow but it will not be like today

Figure 5. The Nature of Reengineered Beliefs

The connecting arrows of the holistic wheel are labeled technology, which includes computer hardware, software, communication networks, service facilities and the like. These technologies are key enablers for creating and implementing the newly designed business process. As such, an integral part of the BPR project is developing or modifying the technology infrastructure in a way that supports, links and aligns all aspects of the business system. It is important to distinguish technology as a business process enabler from technology as the central source of the change. Like many companies, Kodak has improved productivity through the introduction of computer and information technology. However, Kodak has also been guilty of applying technology in a way that "paves the cowpaths." That is, applying technology without first understanding the intent of the process from the customer's perspective. All too often the result is a bad process that is easier to perform. Reengineering requires creative technological insight to take advantage of the true power of technology.

Together, business processes, management systems, jobs and organizational structures, beliefs and behaviors and technology embody the culture of an organization. The concept of culture was coined to represent, in a very broad sense, the qualities of any specific human group that are passed from one generation to the next. In modern organizations culture can be seen at two levels. At the deeper level are the beliefs and behaviors that are shared and passed on over time. These notions about what is important can vary greatly from organization to organization and even within a large organization. While some people care deeply about technological innovation others may focus on pleasing customers. At this level culture can be invisible and, as such, can be very difficult to change. At a more visible level, culture represents the style of an organization that employees are encouraged to follow. For example, people may work long hours, may be conservative in their dress, be outgoing with each other or especially friendly to customers. Because this level is more apparent it is somewhat easier to address, but is still resistant to change in the short term (Kotter, Heskett 1992). Reengineering can not be successful over the long run unless both levels change.

As difficult as it is to change culture, why not concentrate on the more tangible aspects of the reengineering change like work design, technology infrastructure, even office layout, and ignore the culture? Simple, research into organizational change has demonstrated that culture has a profound impact on the effectiveness of an organization. Perhaps the first demonstration of the affect of culture on business results is now commonly referred to as the 'Hawthorne Affect' (Western Electric Company 1939). This research demonstrated that, under the right circumstances, a group of people can quickly form a group identity. And, more significantly, that this identity, or culture, can have a profound positive impact on productivity. In more recent times researchers have demonstrated empirically that culture can have a significant impact on a firm's long-term economic performance. These same researchers have also found that although it is complex and time consuming culture can be changed in a way that enhances performance (Kotter, Heskett 1992). The concepts and the techniques to facilitate this difficult transition are referred to as change management and will be described later in chapter 6.

In summary, do not underestimate the power of your culture. Through the experience of Kodak and many other companies it is clear that attempting to implement a redesigned process into an existing culture will ensure a slow and painful death for that redesigned process.

The second implementation model is the Framework at a Glance (figure 6). It captures on one page, all the major activities required of a total reengineering effort. The methodology behind the framework and described in the following chapters, was developed by Texas Instruments for Kodak practitioners to use in conjunction with BPR teams. While the methodology is not a checklist or cookbook, it does describe a series of activities that have proven to contribute to project success. It can be thought of as a set of best practices, organized in a way that provides order and repeatability to the work. In applying the methodology, Kodak encourages tailoring the activities to meet the specific needs of a project. The methodology has been critical to the success Kodak has had in reengineering since its inception late in 1992. The methodology provides:

- structure to a complex undertaking;
- techniques that are useful in performing the activities; and
- common terminology and understanding of BPR through-out the company.

While each phase of the methodology contains a connected set of activities that make for logical groupings, they can not be considered separate or distinct. In fact, phases may overlap and the BPR team will certainly iterate back and forth between them. At times this may feel like two steps backward for each step forward but such is the nature of a complex undertaking that must be considered in a holistic way.

There are five blocks and one wide arrow that make up the framework at a glance. The four reengineering phases are: project initiation, process understanding, new process design and business transition. They are presented in chapters 2-5, in the order they should be performed on most projects. The first block, forces driving reengineering, is not a reengineering phase, but rather a strategic activity that must be completed either prior to, or in conjunction with initiating a reengineering project. As such, it is discussed in chapter 2 along with project initiation. Along the bottom of the framework at a glance is the change management phase. In this context, change management refers to the people side of the reengineering project and the associated culture. It includes concepts and techniques relating to human resource policy and practice, communication, education and training and organizational development. While the discussion of change management is held until chapter 6, it would be disastrous for a BPR team to assume that the change management work does not begin until the four primary phases are complete.

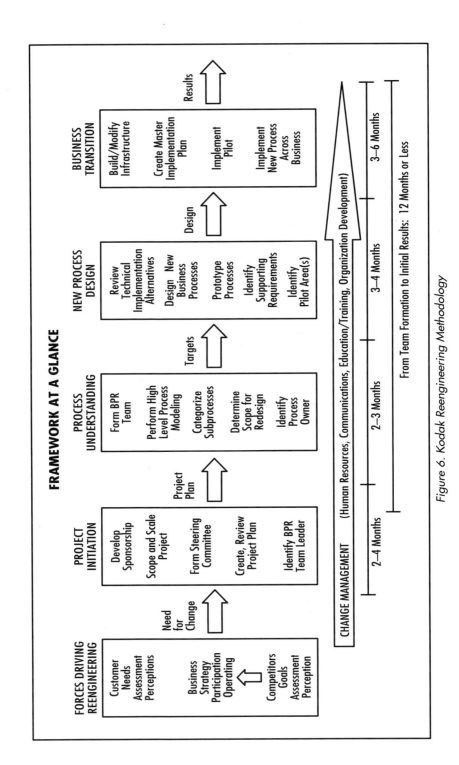

FRAMEWORK AT A GLANCE

FORCES DRIVING REENGINEERING
- Customer Needs Assessment Perceptions
- Business Strategy Participation Operating
- Competitors Goals Assessment Perception

Need for Change

PROJECT INITIATION
- Develop Sponsorship
- Scope and Scale Project
- Form Steering Committee
- Create, Review Project Plan
- Identify BPR Team Leader

Project Plan

PROCESS UNDERSTANDING
- Form BPR Team
- Perform High Level Process Modeling
- Categorize Subprocesses
- Determine Scope for Redesign
- Identify Process Owner

Targets

NEW PROCESS DESIGN
- Review Technical Implementation Alternatives
- Design New Business Processes
- Prototype Processes
- Identify Supporting Requirements
- Identify Pilot Area(s)

Design

BUSINESS TRANSITION
- Build/Modify Infrastructure
- Create Master Implementation Plan
- Implement Pilot
- Implement New Process Across Business

Results

CHANGE MANAGEMENT (Human Resources, Communications, Education/Training, Organization Development)

2–4 Months | 2–3 Months | 3–4 Months | 3–6 Months

From Team Formation to Initial Results: 12 Months or Less

Figure 6. Kodak Reengineering Methodology

Instead, change management must begin the day the idea for reengineering emerges. It is presented last in the hope that by first understanding the total reengineering process you will appreciate the extraordinary need for a well planned, well executed change process.

References

Daniels, Aubrey and Theodore Rosen. 1983. *Performance Management: Improving Quality and Productivity Through Positive Reinforcement.* Performance Management.

Hammer, Michael. 1990. Reengineering work: don't automate, obliterate. *Harvard Business Review.* Vol. 90, no. 4.

Hammer, M. and James Champy. 1993. *Reengineering the Corporation: A Manifesto for Business Revolution.* New York, N.Y.: HarperCollins.

Kotter, John P. and James L. Heskett. 1992. *Corporate Culture and Performance.* Free Press. Greenwich, Conn.: The Free Press.

Western Electric Company, Hawthorne Works. 1939. *Management and the Worker: An Account of a Research Program.* Chicago, Ill.

Project Initiation

Successful project initiation is a key to a successful BPR project. Unlike the phases which follow, omissions or errors made during project initiation tend to compound themselves and are difficult to recover from. Worse yet, the omission or error will probably not emerge until it is too late to do much about it. Hopefully, this knowledge will help you overcome the temptation to shortcut this phase in the name of "getting on with it." Failure to do a thorough job of initiating all aspects of your reengineering project will lead to false starts, frustration, and even abandonment of the project.

The purposes of the project initiation phase are to:

- Ensure that the forces driving the reengineering project are in place and are well understood;
- Develop a case for action for change based on the symptoms that affect the organization or the opportunities that exist for obtaining sustainable competitive advantage;
- Identify the scope and scale of the project, including the processes, functional organizations, product lines, geography and business units involved;
- Identify the key players in the project governance structure including; executive sponsor, process champion, steering committee and team leader, who together will champion the change and help in its implementation; and
- Develop a project plan that includes time and resource requirements.

Forces driving reengineering

What drives an enterprise to reengineer? According to Hammer and Champy (1993) there are three primary factors:

1. The enterprise has *hit the wall* and must reengineer or die. Companies in this mode usually have the motivation to change dramatically, some do not have the time.
2. The enterprise *sees the wall approaching* and is compelled to reengineer to avoid a head-on crash. Companies in this mode probably have many people on both sides of the fence, those that see the opportunity ahead and those that like things to be just as they are.
3. The enterprise wants to *build a higher wall,* making it more difficult for competitors to scale. It is rare indeed to uncover a well established company that has the courage to make fundamental and dramatic changes when things are going well. Those that do invariably have strong, visionary leaders.

Kodak has initiated reengineering projects for all three of these reasons. But, in every case the ultimate reason for reengineering was the customer. In a typical scenario, rising customer expectations exceed the capability of the existing process. For example, a driver of the CI&OM LCGM project was the customer's expectation that they receive product within two days from the time of order placement. The current process was incapable of consistently delivering that level of performance no matter how hard people worked. Since Kodak was already applying continuous improvement techniques in this area and the results were insufficient to meet customer requirements, reengineering was appropriate.

Reengineering projects at Kodak are often driven by the strategic planning process. This management process includes articulation of the business vision and strategy. In this scenario corporate or business unit management either senses a threat — *sees the wall approaching* — or sees an opportunity to gain competitive advantage — *build a higher wall.* The project teams initiated as a result of this process have a high probability for success since the business strategy is clear and management involvement is strong from the start.

Even when reengineering projects are not driven directly by the formal strategic planning process, a business strategy is still critical to success. A reengineering team may proceed successfully through the project initiation phase and even through the process understanding phase, but without a strategy things will unravel during new process design. At that point the team will begin to ask questions about the future of the business. What business do we want to be in? What core competencies do we want to develop and take advantage of? What markets do we want to serve? If the answers to these questions are less than clear, or don't exist at all, time is wasted and frustration abounds.

A structured strategic planning process for evaluating market forces, determining gaps and initiating projects is valid and perhaps preferred. However, there are times when the enterprise has hit the wall and a reengineering project is born out of the passion of a single fanatical individual. If this fanatic also has a clear vision, effective communication skills and a level of positional authority, a powerful combination exists for reengineering success.

Developing the case for action
Typically, commissioning a reengineering project includes the appointment of a team leader and a reengineering practitioner. Together, with the initiating process champion, the three work to further specify the project and create the initial case for action.

The case for action is a simple, but powerful document that clearly and concisely articulates the need for dramatic improvement from the customer's perspective. It becomes the basis upon which the entire project unfolds. It is the foundation upon which the BPR team will build a stake for the project, develop design ideas and evaluate the ultimate success of the prototype and pilot. It must convey two key messages:

1. This is how we look in the eyes of our customer; and
2. This is what we must become.

At the same time, the case for action must provide a vision that people can rally around. People will need justification for undertaking such a demanding task as reengineering. One test of the power of the case for action is the degree to which it triggers emotion with the stakeholders. Whether it be fear or excitement, if the case for action does not elicit an emotional response, either the problem being addressed is trivial or the message is unclear. An effective case for action should include six major elements (Hammer and Champy 1993). These six elements can be clearly seen in figure 1.

---

1) The *business context* summarizes what has changed in the environment.
 The commercial graphics market has become increasingly competitive. Growth has slowed to 1% per year, creating a battle over existing customers. This has resulted in price pressure on the total industry supply chain, squeezing margins for suppliers like us.

2) The *business problem* states the source of the organizations concerns.
 Customer order management problems are slow to be resolved and result in significant intervention by the sales force. This reduces the time they have to follow new leads and grow revenue.

3) The *demands of the marketplace* describes how customer expectations require new performance capabilities.
 Customers expect a perfectly reliable source of supply with quick delivery and no back-orders. Moreover, each customer wants a supplier to consider their collective needs and provide integrated solutions.

4) The *diagnostics* section explains why the current capabilities and business processes are unable to meet the new demands of the marketplace.
 Our current business processes were designed in a time when the graphics industry was growing and most customers had similar needs. Today's customers have unique needs and our processes hinder our ability to deal with those needs effectively.

5) The *cost of inaction* warns of the consequences of continuing with the status quo.
 Continuing on the path we are on will result in reduced market share in a declining market. If we are to win over the long term we must take market share from our competitors.

6) Finally the case for action should include two or three far reaching *quantitative objectives* that the reengineered enterprise must deliver. Obviously, to be credible these objectives must be derived from the facts described in the previous five sections.
 We must provide customers with immediate access to product and service information. Customer requirements must be processed completely with a single contact. We must reduce the cycle time to complete a customer order by 67% and increase orders completed via a single customer contact call by 300%.

Figure 1. CI&OM LCGM: Case for Action

 In summary, the benefits of a clear, concise and compelling case for action are that it provides:

 • A definition of the situation in a way that stakeholders can see the problem from the customer perspective;

- A basis for team decisions with respect to the redesign; and
- A rallying point for the future of the enterprise.

Establishing scope and scale
The *scope* is defined by the sub-processes included in the effort. (A sub-process is simply a process a level of detail below the major processes.) The scope must encompass enough of the organization's business processes to address the major customer issues. To illustrate let's continue with the CI&OM LCGM example.

In establishing the scope the team had to consider which of the business sub-processes were in the most need of redesign in order to meet customer needs. The team knew from customer sight visits, surveys and Kodak sales people that cycle time was a key customer concern. But the team needed to understand more specifically which cycle was an issue. They learned through additional sessions with customers that the concern centered around the order-delivery cycle. The process model, which describes the project scope, is illustrated in figure 2.

The team described this scope as follows: all customer interface and order management sub-processes, from the time a customer has an application need, until customer satisfaction is verified.

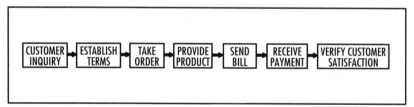

Figure 2. LCGM Interface and Order Management Process

In a company as large and diverse as Kodak, similar business processes exist in several different businesses and across a number of geographic regions. CI&OM for example, can be found repeated in each of the regions around the world. Establishing the scale sets the boundaries relative to which geographic regions, product lines, businesses and customer segments should be included in the BPR project. However, scale cannot be determined independent of scope. Because project complexity is a function of the scope and the scale, both must be considered simultaneously. Since complexity tends to drive the resources required, both in terms of number and duration, and resources are in most cases limited, the trade-offs can be difficult.

The steps for establishing scope and scale are:

1. Establish the scope so that the project boundaries are wide enough to address a significant customer concern.
2. Identify the ideal scale by selecting the region, product lines, business units and geographies to be included.
3. Identify the resources available for the reengineering effort.
4. Consider the resulting complexity of the total project given the preferred scope and scale, and estimate the resources required to complete each phase of the reengineering project.
5. Test the resources required against the resources available.
6. Repeat steps 2-5 until a match exists between resources required and resources available.
7. If a match cannot be made by reducing scale as a last resort, return to step 1 and reduce scope.

In the CI&OM LCGM project there were three key variables relating to scale: the customer segments, the geographic region and the products and services.

The customer segment options were:

• Small businesses
• Newspapers
• Specialty product users
• Large commercial graphics

The geographic areas considered were:

• Worldwide
• United States and Canada only

The products and services considered were:

• All Kodak products and services
• Kodak Imaging products and services only
• A subset of Kodak Imaging products and services

After many iterations through the seven-step scoping and scaling process the team settled on, and the sponsor supported a scale that included all Kodak Imaging products of interest to the large commercial graphics customer segment in the United States and Canada. This scale specifically excludes some customer segments and some regions of the world. This was done so the resources available could progress at a pace that would enable them to begin implementation in 12 months or less. The 12-month limit was set because the team felt significant results were critical within the traditional annual budgeting cycle.

Establishing the scope and scale is an important step because it sets the boundaries and implies the organizations and people that will be involved. Knowing the stakeholders early on is critical to a successful change management effort and hence a successful reengineering effort. However, the team, the sponsor and the steering committee must be open to modification of the scope and scale as new information surfaces.

Establishing project governance structure

The power of the reengineering methodology is in the way it brings together many concepts and techniques. Integration of these concepts and techniques can be complex and will require the best people you have. Not the best people *available*, but the best people you have. Therefore, establishing the governance structure and selecting the BPR team is a critical and often politically challenging step. It is also, perhaps the first opportunity to test the commitment of the enterprise to reengineering. When the enterprise makes available its best people, despite the pain that extracting them from their current role creates, it is likely that the commitment is real.

The project governance structure (figure 3) identifies five roles that must be filled for every reengineering project.

1. The *executive sponsor* must have the power, either through position or personal influence, to endorse and drive implementation of the new design across the entire scope and scale of the project. Typically, the executive sponsor is from one of the organizations at the core of the business process being redesigned. This is the person that must articulate the vision to the project stakeholders. The executive sponsor must have the wherewithal to provide resources and the courage to resolve disputes by whatever means necessary. Characteristics include, credibility with the people that are part of the change and a willingness to live with ambiguity as the project unfolds.

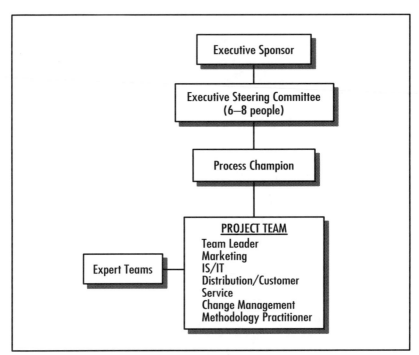

Figure 3. CI&OM LCGM Governance Structure

2. The *process champion* is one of the key leaders of the change process. Characteristics include: credibility with the sponsor, the steering committee, the BPR team and the affected organizations, understanding of both the processes within the reengineering scope, and the reengineering methodology. This individual must also be able to devote significant personal effort, at key times as much as 30 percent of their work week. How do you find your process champion? Sometimes the process champion is obvious very early on, either because they were one of the project initiators, or they were appointed by the executive sponsor. Other times, the process champion emerges as the project moves through the project initiation phase. In the worst case the process champion must be recruited in the classic sense. That is, identifying the qualified people from throughout the enterprise and making a case for the opportunity that the reengineering project presents.

3. As the name implies the *team leader* must have the ability to mold a group of diverse, energetic, sometimes non-conforming individuals into a high performing team. Implicit in this are: group process leadership skills and an understanding of the BPR methodology.

In Kodak's experience the team leader is a key link between the project and the many stakeholders. Therefore, the ability to communicate effectively at all levels is essential. When identifying your potential team leaders look for people that have a history of driving change and are known for their persistence under trying circumstances.

4. The *executive steering committee* is a group of 6-8 people that provides support and guidance and removes barriers for the BPR team. They often influence the direction of the redesign, and must collectively have the authority, and willingness to take personal responsibility for its successful implementation. As such, the group is made up of influential people representing a majority of the project scope and scale. The CI&OM LCGM project steering committee included stakeholders from the primary business unit and from the functional organizations currently performing the CI&OM processes for the LCGM. Ideally, a steering committee would also have a customer representative. This might be a current customer, or a customer surrogate by way of a sales representative that has a strong affiliation with the customer.

5. The *reengineering practitioner* is uniquely positioned to play the role of change agent. As an internal consultant the change agent has four primary roles (Hunsaker 1982):

- Catalyst — When acting as a catalyst the practitioner looks for opportunities to upset the status quo in a way that brings renewed energy to the problem.
- Solution giver — In this role the practitioner has a chance to apply design ideas, often learned from previous work, to the reengineering design. While this role can be very valuable it can compromise the balance between solution giver and process leader. Therefore the practitioner must be careful how and when solutions are contributed.
- Resource linker — In this role the practitioner brings in others with relevant expertise to apply to the problem at hand.
- Process leader — This is a critical role that all practitioners must always play. In this capacity the practitioner works closely with the team leader to bring reengineering process expertise to the team. In this role the practitioner is the source of group process techniques. Although there are many techniques the three most often used are:

1. FAST diagramming — is useful in creating the high level map during the project initiation phase, and again in creating the detailed design in the new process design phase. An important contribution this technique makes is in the process naming conventions it requires. The technique suggests using one verb and one noun to name each process. Following this protocol results in models that are succinct, easy to communicate and interpret.

2. Pareto analysis — is a simple and effective approach to identifying priorities and for making team decisions. It is useful in all phases of the project.

3. Timeboxing — is a project management technique that can help keep the reengineering team moving quickly and delivering on commitments. The name comes from the way activities are framed or boxed. Each activity is defined with a clear set of deliverables and a firm due date. The work is planned to fit within the box and is continuously reevaluated to ensure that the expectations are met. This approach can keep the BPR team from becoming mired in unnecessary detail.

The practitioner's knowledge and experience with these and other group process techniques enables the team to deliver high quality deliverables in an efficient manner. Experienced practitioners might also become a coach and confidant to the team leader, helping the team leader with the subtleties of managing change, effective team leadership and communication style. Finally, the practitioner provides an outsider's viewpoint that other team members, entrenched in the current process and its culture, might not. Such a diverse set of requirements calls for an individual with:

- Process orientation;
- Great patience;
- Team building experience;
- Group process leadership experience;
- Experience in many group process techniques;
- Business orientation;
- Information technology knowledge; and
- Knowledge of other experts and a willingness to use their talents.

Developing the project plan

With the initial scope and scale established and the case for action drafted, the work ahead and the time available to complete it starts to become clear. A preliminary project plan is needed to organize the activities and align the resources. In most cases great detail is not needed at this time. A simple one or two-page project plan should include, resource requirements, the overall schedule, key deliverables and major milestones.

In creating this project plan often the original scope and scale is tested as trade-offs are made between schedule requirements and available resources. Now is not the time to dramatically scale back the effort. Reengineering projects tend to demand twice as much work in half the time of a typical project. There are at least three reasons for this. The first is that a fast pace tends to keep the project team from becoming entrenched in unnecessary detail. Second, the business cannot afford to have 6 to 10 people, plus part or all of the management team reengineering processes for very long, when those are the very same people that must serve the customer. And, third, the business either sees the wall, or is already up against it and, as such, requires a new process sooner rather than later. In driving the project to completion in a time frame that is much faster than your cultural paradigm would expect, dedication and hard work must be combined with strong leadership and effective project management.

For example, the CI&OM LCGM project established completion dates for each of the four project phases: project initiation, process understanding, new process design and business transition. The BPR team timeboxed each phase and treated each date as a "drop dead" date. Meaning, trade-offs were made with regard to the level of detail and the resources applied. To reinforce the commitment to the agreed upon dates, the team established reviews with the steering committee on each milestone's due date. The team was limited to nine people so the only flexibility was in level of detail and hours worked. By limiting the level of detail and working long hours a key milestone was never missed.

With all the expectations surrounding the BPR effort the demand for quick results is extraordinary. Michael Hammer suggests a maximum 12-month time frame from team start to initial results, but Kodak is typically driving for half that, sometimes less. While committing to a reengineering project brings with it some personal sacrifice, Kodak is not interested in burning out its best people. To avoid this, great care is taken in defining scope and scale, and timeboxing to limit unnecessary detail. At the same time, the ability of the BPR team to interact in a high-performing way will result in quicker decision making. A useful team ground rule that can contribute to team efficiency is the Pareto 80% rule. In this application any team member can at anytime, suggest that the topic on the table has been discussed to the point where the team is in 80% agreement, or has achieved 80% of the value out of the discussion. If the team agrees, the decision is made and the discussion ends.

Lessons learned: project initiation

1. If a business strategy does not exist, do not pass go. Attempting to proceed beyond process understanding without a well understood business strategy is pointless. Designing a new process demands not only an understanding of customer requirements, but also of the business objectives.
2. If a business strategy does exist, but it is unclear, work with management to articulate it in parallel with the project initiation phase. It is critical for the BPR team to have deep understanding of the business strategy prior to new process design, and for the affected organizations to understand it prior to business transition.
3. If your organization is large and there are multiple reengineering efforts underway at the same time establish an exchange meeting to learn from each other. This can enable one team to build on the experiences of other teams, avoiding pitfalls, improving quality and perhaps progressing more quickly.
4. If a strong project sponsor does not exist, spare people unnecessary frustration, do not form the team until one emerges or is recruited. Much activity can take place without a sponsor and the enterprise may even feel it is making good progress. Without a strong, dedicated sponsor it is so much hand waving.
5. It is useful to test the boundaries early and often to ensure that everyone involved truly understands the potentially dramatic changes that will result, both personally and organizationally. If this is not done early it will come up during the business transition phase, at a time when the issues will be difficult or impossible to deal with.
6. Structure the project in a way that ensures the sponsor has "skin in the game." That is, project success must be at least as important to the sponsor as it will certainly become to the BPR team. Perhaps

the simplest way to do this is to recruit the sponsor from an organization within the scope and scale of the BPR project.

7. Engage the sponsor in communicating the vision and the case for action to other stakeholders. Two good things result. One, the sponsor reinforces their own commitment to the change. Two, the stakeholders see an important leader speaking positively, even fervently about the reengineering project, thereby building their commitment.

8. Check your project objectives. Are they far reaching and specific? Keep them posted for the team to reference at all times.

9. Provide opportunities for the sponsor to learn the role by interacting with other reengineering sponsors, both within and outside the firm.

10. When determining customers needs:

    * spend time face to face, preferably on their turf;
    * focus on their business and their needs, not on their opinion of your operations; and
    * interview insiders that have direct customer contact (sales, customer service, order entry, etc.). They often have great insight. This has the added benefit of engaging them as change agents in support of the reengineering effort.

11. Spend time understanding the improvement efforts already underway across the enterprise. Determine the future of each with respect to the reengineering project. At worst they will be in direct conflict with the BPR effort, even if not they are likely to have the kind of people the BPR effort will require.

12. Establish a few key milestones and do not deviate from them. Consistently delivering on predetermined dates will build confidence within the team and credibility with stakeholders.

13. Establish an aggressive project timeline; besides achieving benefits sooner, the sense of urgency keeps the team focused.

References

Hammer, Michael and James Champy. 1993. *Reengineering the Corporation: A Manifesto for Business Revolution.* New York, N.Y.: HarperCollins.

Hunsaker, Phillip L. 1982. *Strategies for Organizational Change: Role of the Inside Change Agent.* Englewood Cliffs, N.J.: Prentice Hall.

Process Understanding

The overall goal of the process understanding phase is to understand the current process, in terms of inputs, work performed, and outputs and measures, well enough to design a new process that will meet customer needs.

Performing the following activities is key to building process understanding for the team and the stakeholders:

- Form the business process reengineering team. This is the team that will perform most of the work in the process understanding and new process design phases.
- Build the high level business process model which will be used to help build understanding of the process for the team and the stakeholders.
- Test the scope and scale that was initially defined in project initiation. With all that has been learned throughout process understanding is it still appropriate?
- Identify the process owner who, as the title suggests, will eventually own the responsibility for delivering the output of the new process.

Understanding, not analyzing

Perhaps the biggest challenge of the process understanding phase is avoiding a disease which can kill a reengineering project: paralysis via analysis. In the words of Dr. Hammer, "The difference between process understanding and process analysis is about 16 weeks." The practitioner can help prevent this disease through active group facilitation, sound project management techniques and efficient distribution of the workload.

An efficient way to distribute the work of the team is to structure parallel work flow sub teams (figure 1). These teams are made up primarily of members of the BPR team, but may include experts as well.

EXTERNAL	CUSTOMER	INTERNAL	CHANGE
Benchmark CI&OM	ID needs (macro)	Measure current results	Assess culture
	ID needs (detail)		Develop plan
Analyze environment	Customer direction	Categorize sub-processes	Team training
Technology trends	Plan customer visits	Process modeling	Stakeholder assessment
Establish metrics		ID strengths, weaknesses	Project team perf appraisal
		Current system analysis	

Figure 1. CI&OM LCGM Sub-Team Structure

1. *External sub team*—Responsible for process and metric benchmarking, conducting an environmental analysis and investigating relevant technology trends.
2. *Customer sub team* — Responsible for identifying customer needs and the direction of the industry within which the customer competes. The team also has responsibility for arranging involvement of all team members in the customer assessment process.
3. *Internal sub team* — Responsible for investigating the current performance level of the business process. This may require establishing some short term measurement systems to determine the baseline. The internal team takes responsibility for updating the high level process model. If appropriate, this sub team also performs a scan of the existing information systems supporting the process, especially the interfaces to other systems and processes.
4. *Change management sub team* — Responsible for assessing the current environment and identifying the key resistance points. Also, responsible for developing and driving the change manage-

ment plan for stakeholders, as well as for BPR team members. Unlike the other three teams, this team has significant responsibilities throughout the entire reengineering project.

A note about team dynamics with respect to these sub teams. Each sub team must be fully empowered to carry out its responsibilities if the parallel work structure is to be time efficient. That means, when a sub team has completed a task it delivers its learnings and conclusions to the full BPR team. This is very different from reporting back with a ideas or proposals which the BPR team then debates and decides upon. Adopting this can be a new, and at times difficult way of working for the project team. However, it will be well worth the effort as your sub teams take on their tasks with increased energy and the pace of your reengineering projects exceed all expectations.

Forming the BPR team
A BPR team, made up of business insiders — those performing the current processes, including both managers and doers — and outsiders — those not directly involved in the current process such as, reengineering practitioners, human resource experts and customers, — is formed early in this phase. The team leader, process champion and practitioner identify the capabilities required to design a new process that will meet customer needs within the defined scope and scale. Once the capability requirements are clear candidates can be evaluated. Team member capabilities that Kodak has found critical are: ability to take the customer's perspective, desire to work in a team environment, optimism in the face of adversity and determination to succeed. Besides these capabilities the team needs people that can provide insight on the current process, balanced with one or two people that have an outsider perspective with respect to the process. The ratio that seems to work well is three insiders to each outsider.

By selecting the most respected individuals from the various job types, the team will have credibility with a wide range of stakeholders, even before they deliver at their first milestone. An obvious problem with selecting these highly respected individuals is that they will already be 110% busy with other meaningful work. A rule of thumb: if it is easy for an organization to give up an individual to the BPR team, the person is probably not the one the team needs. This inherent conflict may become a test of the power and commitment of the sponsor and the process champion.

A few additional points relative to team formation. Because reengineering requires radical thinking Kodak has tried to instill radical thinking in the team processes. One small, yet significant tactic is to form and operate the BPR team in a way that is very different from a typical improvement team. That starts with team selection. Rather than be concerned with ensuring that all affected organizations are represented on the team, consider only the capabilities required and bring in the people that best match those requirements. Further, you may want to employ a "skunk works" approach. Skunk works is a way to set up a project team where all team members are located together, preferably away from their normal day-to-day workplace. It usually means that the team is full-time, or as close to full-time as possible, on the project. It also means that the ground rules the team operates by are different from the traditional project team ground rules. Simple examples are a different dress code, or not subjecting the team to formal management approval processes. These are just two of the little things you can do to establish the environment that will encourage the team to think in new ways about existing situations. Your culture may be different so other techniques may have more impact. In any case, be bold right from the start.

A final point about team selection. The availability of a potential team member is usually dependent on the amount of time the project requires. That is, if the reengineering team does not require too much time the individual can probably be made available. The closer the commitment is to full-time the less willing organization managers are to give up their best people. In many cases the urgency for results will demand a dedicated, full-time team. Other times the trade off with other commitments must be balanced. The trick is to be realistic about the amount of time the team needs to work on the project given the scope, scale and the time available. In any case, a team that is dedicated less than 50 percent of their work week will have difficulty making steady progress. And, a full-time team should never take on part-time members. The momentum lost by continually bringing the part-timers up to speed will slow progress and frustrate all involved.

Building the high level process model
A high level process model (HLPM) is a representation of the business with two characteristics that separate it from other process flow charts and especially from the traditional, hierarchical organization chart.

1. It is focused on the customer. That does not mean it starts and ends with a customer, but that it is centered on the customer's process.
2. It is business process oriented. Instead of names of organization, such as manufacturing or distribution, a HLPM depicts the business processes that support the customer's process.

The objectives of creating a high level model of the business process are:

- Build a common understanding among the team and other stakeholders;
- Encourage a common vocabulary that cuts across functional and organizational boundaries;
- Highlight the sub-processes critical to achieving customer needs;
- Test the boundaries established by the initial scope and scale;
- Identify key interface points; and
- Pinpoint redundancies and other forms of wasted effort.

A high level process model starts with the customer's process and identifies the major sub-processes in support of that customer process. As the name implies, at this point only a high level model is required. However, what is high level to one team member or stakeholder group may be a trivial detail to another. The challenge is knowing how much detail to include in the process model. The answer of course is, it depends. As much as anything, it depends on the detail needed to meet the objectives of the HLPM stated above. At the same time, as with every step, change management is an issue. If, for example, a critical stakeholder feels the model is incomplete because it does not show a particular sub-process and adding the sub-process does not detract from the model, by all means add it.

Following are some principles to keep in mind, which will help the team develop the HLPM efficiently.

- The model is designed to facilitate understanding, not for problem analysis.
- Simple is better than complex. Corollary — less detail is better than more detail.
- The HLPM should have about 6 and certainly no more than 15 major sub-processes from start to finish.

- Taping notes to a conference room wall is an ideal way to start. It's tactile that it involves people, is highly visible and is inexpensive.

The FAST diagramming technique described in chapter 2 can assist the team in building a model that is concise and understandable. In applying this technique sub-processes are defined with one verb and one noun. For example, write order and deliver product. The result is a simple, succinct model that is easy to communicate and interpret.

A question that often comes up is, "Is the HLPM a picture of what exists today or is it depicting the future state?" Not an easy question to answer because it is both. That is, it is a process oriented model of what exists today. It models what is, but does it in terms of process, rather than organization structure. By its very nature this new way of thinking tends to move everyone a step closer to the future state.

The HLPM becomes level 1 in a layered series of levels that provide further detail to each sub-process at the time it is needed. Typically level 2, which would include a one-page description of each box depicted on the HLPM, is needed in order to identify the process owner. The next level of detail, level 3, may be needed prior to prototype. Finally, level 4, which would be the most specific, might be needed to implement across the business.

Identifying and implementing quick hits

As understanding of the process develops, opportunities for improving the existing process will surface. Since you are charged with reengineering and not with continuous improvement, what do you do? The potential downside to addressing every good improvement opportunity is the team might divert its attention away from the primary effort or could implement a change that will become obsolete when the reengineered process is implemented. On the other hand, if there is money to be saved or other desirable benefits that can be realized quickly you don't want to let those lie until the entire redesign is developed and rolled out. The reengineering methodology refers to these opportunities as quick hits. A quick hit is a simple, quick fix to eliminate an obvious error or to upgrade the existing process. Implementing a quick hit can have great value for a number of reasons:

- It can build credibility for the team as others realize that the team is not only studying and planning, but is doing things at the same time.
- It can make the team feel good about itself. There is nothing like a success for building confidence and future successes.
- It can lead to self-funding for the team. The idea is for the team to deliver savings from quick hits that are equivalent to the cost of operating the team.

A CI&OM example of a successful quick hit emerged while the team was visiting customers. They found that sales people were spending time each day recording their customer visits for the day. Each week the forms were sent to a central location and entered into a computer database. The sales people generally did not see added value from their perspective but provided the input so their managers could evaluate how frequently customers were being called on. In interviewing the managers the BPR team found that most of them had stopped using the database because they had other means of determining how well a customer location was being served. Clearly, the process output no longer served the purpose for which it was originally designed. An obvious quick hit opportunity. In the long term everyone agreed there was value in having a quantitative means for understanding how well each customer was being served and the process needed redesign. However, in the short term, the company could save some time for the sales people, some data entry labor and some computer time by shutting down the current process. That is exactly what was done.

In conclusion, quick hits can have great benefits but they must be carefully selected and executed so as not to divert the team from its primary task.

Verifying the scope of the redesign
During project initiation the initial scope and scale was established. However, much has been learned through self examination, environmental scanning and especially customer visits. At this point the team and the key stakeholders reassess the initial scope and scale based on this new information. Only by working through this learning process will the team and the key stakeholders have a strong sense for the sub-processes that must be redesigned to satisfy customer needs. To accomplish this re-scoping the team works through exactly the same seven-step process that led it to the original scope and scale. This activity illustrates the iterative nature of the reengineering process.

Identifying the process owner
The process owner is the person that will take responsibility for the new business process and will be held accountable for the results of the process. The more the process owner is involved in the design of the new process the smoother the transition to process owner will be. Therefore, identifying this individual prior to redesign will allow for this early process design interaction.

How does one find a process owner? In some cases the process champion will evolve into the process owner role. That is the easy way and may be preferred since the process champion has the background, commitment and likely the appropriate characteristics. If that is not the case, a person with strong leadership skills, credibility and process orientation must be recruited. Recruitment may be done by the sponsor, the team leader, the steering committee, or better yet, by all three. During this recruitment process look for an individual with all the aforementioned characteristics, plus a willingness and ability to make the transition from functionally aligned leadership to process aligned leadership. This transition will probably be made even more difficult for the newly appointed process owners because they will be required to maintain two roles: one that manages the existing organization and the other that leads the process. The process owner must have the energy and patience to carry out both roles until the structure of the entire enterprise realigns around business processes.

The sponsor and the BPR team must work with the process owner to build process understanding and commitment. In addition to bringing the process owner up to speed on the project and the new design, the process owner must learn what being a process owner means. In most companies the term process owner is entirely new and the job responsibilities rather foreign. This can be accomplished through coaching from an owner of another process, the sponsor, the team leader or the practitioner.

Lessons learned: process understanding

1. As process understanding progresses new stakeholders will emerge. The needs of each stakeholder must be incorporated into the thinking of the team and dealt with proactively.
2. Carefully select one or two quick hits, spin them off to another team or implement them quickly, then get the BPR team back to the primary task of reengineering the business. This can build

credibility that the BPR team because it is "doing something" without diverting too much energy.

3. Document, understand and deal with the ongoing improvement projects underway in the organization within the redesign scope and scale. Often these projects have strong supporters and if not dealt with here can undermine the business transition effort. These teams are also an important source of people that advocate change.

4. The BPR team must include one or two people that know the current business processes well and are respected by their peers. Without these insiders the credibility of the project team will always be in doubt.

5. A full-time team works better, faster, more efficiently and in the long run costs less than a part-time team. If you can't pull that off do not attempt to mix part-time and full-time people on the same team. It will lead to frustration for all involved.

6. The best people will probably be difficult to recruit. After all, they are the best people and are already doing important work. Often, this is the first test of the commitment of the enterprise to the reengineering effort.

7. Team co-location is a simple, yet effective way to greatly enhance communication and improve team dynamics.

8. Every person on the team should experience some form of customer interaction prior to new process design. The obvious reason is to ensure a customer focused redesign. Less obvious, is the credibility it will bring to the proposed redesign.

9. At the conclusion of process understanding having documented a high level process model is important; having a perfect process model is not. Get it on paper, or better yet on the wall and upgrade and refine it as the project progresses.

10. Provide opportunities for key stakeholders to review, understand and upgrade the process model as a way to build stakeholder commitment.

New Process Design

Without a doubt, the early steps of new process design are the most exciting for the BPR team. All the stage setting, data gathering, customer interviews and stake building lead up to this pivotal phase. It's likely that your team will be so anxious that many informal, preliminary redesign discussions will occur prior to this time. Those discussions can be productive as long as they do not deter from the work at hand and the redesign ideas do not become "etched in stone" prior to this new process design phase.

The activities which will lead to a powerful design:

- Reviewing technology alternatives to expand the team's technological perspective and introduce potential design ideas.
- Designing the new process. Kodak has evolved a six-step group process which will lead to a customer focused design.
- Prototyping the new design involves creating a way to test the design before it goes live.
- Identifying the scope, scale, location and timing of the initial pilot.

Reviewing technology alternatives

The new process design phase starts with a review of technology alternatives. This does not mean that technology is the focal point of the new process design, but that technology enables the process. Technology, particularly information technology, applied to a broken process fixes nothing and may even make future process change more difficult. However, there is clearly a significant role for technology in the design process. Technology can fuel the team's creative process as it creates the new design. For example, in the CI&OM LCGM project the team considered what electronic data interchange (EDI) could do to achieve the objectives of the new process. Indeed, they found a key role for EDI as a process enabler. Moreover, they were able to design elements of the process around the EDI capability, literally changing the way the work was done because of the capability the technology delivered. In summary, expand the teams technological horizons during the redesign phase, but do not allow technology to become the focal point of the new design, or force technology on the existing process.

Designing the new business process
The challenge in the new process design phase, is to turn large volumes of data into useful information. Much of the data will be qualitative in the form of customer interviews, market research surveys, benchmarking descriptions, environmental assessments, technological capabilities and the like. A technique is required which will bring structure to this data, while at the same time provide freedom for the team to be highly creative. The technique which follows is one Kodak has developed from the field of strategy development and used with great success in this situation.

1. *Hold integration meeting* — Often for efficiency, the data gathering that occurs in the process understanding phase is divided among team members and executed in parallel. This means that each team member may have a slightly, or even significantly different view of the issues and opportunities. The integration meeting is a session for each team member to share what they have learned with other team members. The purpose is not necessarily to create a common mindset, but to allow everyone to adequately understand all relevant input. Depending on the scope and scale this meeting can take from two hours to two days. The session needs capable facilitation to keep it focused and effective. This can be done by agreeing to a common presentation format and limiting discussion to clarification of the information presented. The practitioner must not allow the session to turn into a debate of the information presented or into a problem solving discussion.

2. *Hold issues meeting* — The issues meeting should take place within a day or two of the integration meeting. By so doing the team will have had enough time to reflect on what they have heard but not so much that they have forgotten any of it. The session starts with a team brain storming of the key issues. A way to steer the brainstorming in the right direction is to ask a question like, "From a customer's perspective what is the biggest issue we face over the next 3-5 years?" Similar questions from a supplier and stakeholder perspective will result in a rather lengthy list of issues. This list can then be prioritized using a simple technique like Pareto analysis. The objective is to bring out the 8-12 issues that are most critical to meeting the objectives stated in the case for action.

3. *Develop redesign table* — Now that everyone has a common understanding and the issues have surfaced and been prioritized, it is time to get really creative. How will the enterprise deal with the key issues? At this time the objective is to obtain a macro redesign. That is one that is at a high level but has enough detail that the stakeholders can envision what life would be like in the future state. Start by stating each issue as a question. For example, if long delivery cycle time is one of the key issues the question might read, "What can we do to significantly reduce delivery cycle time?" Working with this one issue the team can use a variety of creative group process techniques to identify many alternatives. (*A Kick in the Seat of the Pants*, Roger von Oech 1986, is one good source of creative group process techniques.) This pattern repeats for each of the key issues. The results can be neatly organized in a table, hence the name redesign table. An example of a completed redesign table from CI&OM LCGM is shown in figure 1.

4. *Establish selection criteria* — The next obvious step might be to select the best option from each column. However, doing so could create an elegant design that might not meet the objectives, or solve the problems stated in the case for action. A step to establish selection criteria is needed. Identify the critical few criteria by which the design alternatives can be evaluated. Most of the criteria should be drawn from the case for action.

5. *Identify redesign themes* — With the criteria in hand the BPR team can identify any number of themes by selecting one option from each of the columns in the redesign table. The next step is to name the themes and associate a brief description of the theme. Examples of

WHAT ARE WE TRYING TO DO FOR EK	WHAT ARE WE TRYING TO DO FOR CONSUMER	CHANNEL NEEDS	HORIZONTAL INTEGRATION	VERTICAL INTEGRATION	APPROACH TO JOB DESIGN
Drive Top Line Sales	Maximize Flexibility	Collaborate To Provide Services	Maintain/ Preserve Product Alignment	Respond Only To Critical Needs	One Empowered Person Capable of Handling Many Functions
Reduce Internal Costs	Allow For Maximum Margins	We Do It All (CIOM)			Team Can Handle Many Functions
Increase Profitability (2 Years)	Collaborate To Make You More Competitive	They Do It All	Maximize Market Segment Alignment	Alliances Maximize Control Through Ownership	Case Manager With Supporting Teams
Increase Cash Flow	High Value, Full Service	Flexibility			
Competitive Weapon					Reliance on Functional Experts
Optimize Return On Assets					

INFORMATION			
INTENSITY	INTEGRATION	USERS	TIMELINESS
High	High	EK/Channel/ Consumers/Suppliers	Real Time
Moderate	Moderate	EK/Channel	On Line
Low	Low	EK Only	Batch

Figure 1. CI&OM LCGM Redesign Table

themes are Low Cost, Expansion or Growth, Maximum Value, etc. Creating three or more themes will stretch the team to be creative in the way it combines options from each column of the redesign table. Multiple themes will also be important in communicating with stakeholders, as it provides them more of an opportunity to engage in the thought processes of the team.

6. *Score each theme* - Finally, each theme can be evaluated and scored relative to the criteria. A weighted scoring model is a technique that works well here. To develop the weighted scoring model assign a weight to each criteria according to importance in the eyes of the customer. Then, one design theme at a time, evaluate the merits of the design with respect to the criteria and assign a score. Multiply the score by the weight for each criteria, and sum the products. The CI&OM LCGM team developed three themes, scored them and selected a theme they called the "Weapon" theme. This theme scored relatively high and more importantly passed the subjective test of the BPR team. That is, it felt right.

The redesign table can be a very powerful device for communicating the macro redesign. It will also become the focal point and the framework for developing the detail design needed to prototype.

Creating the macro redesign and sharing it with stakeholders is exciting and emotional. In contrast creating the detail design can be arduous. It is a matter of working each element of the redesign theme, with respect to the holistic wheel. For example, one of the columns on the CI&OM LCGM redesign table is labeled "channel needs." The Weapon theme identified "Collaborate to provide services" as the option of choice. Of course they had a brief description of what that meant in order to explain it consistently to all stakeholders, but that was it. For the team to move forward more detail was needed. So they took the concept and asked themselves what it meant with respect to business processes, jobs and organizational structure, management systems, beliefs and behaviors and technology. As they were doing this work they kept these guidelines in mind:

- Design for speed;
- Ensure each piece of work is performed only once;
- Build quality into the work;
- Keep it simple; and
- Design jobs so that one person can complete a meaningful piece of work for a customer.

With these basic rules and the redesign table the team successfully designed and documented the next level of detail.

It is also a good idea at this point to begin to involve some of the process performers. Their involvement will help ensure that no important elements are missed and perhaps more importantly will begin to solidify their understanding and commitment to the new design.

Prototyping the process
Once a redesign theme has the support of key stakeholders and the level 2 process modeling and design detail has been developed it is time to test it out. This testing or prototyping is a way to evaluate the design in a safe, non-production environment. However, before planning and executing the prototype there is yet another scoping and scaling decision to be made. Once again, the question to answer is, "With the resources and time available how much of the total project scope and scale is it practical to prototype?" Now the trade-offs

get even more difficult since the risk involved in not prototyping part of the scope and scale can be significant.

Let's return to the CI&OM LCGM example. The team recognized that time and resources were such that prototyping over the entire scope and scale was impractical. They also concluded that some elements of the redesign were low risk from a customer perspective, making prototyping a luxury. Finally, they reminded themselves that there was always the pilot to work out any final bugs. With that logic the team elected to prototype an element of their redesign called case team. The case team is the group that will serve as the single source of customer contact to Kodak for LCGM customers. The design called for co-location of experts from all the organizations currently involved in customer interface. Simple on paper, complex in execution. What makes it complex is that each function currently has its own protocol for dealing with customers, its own information databases and a rather narrow frame of reference and skill set. To create a true case team all those things needed to change in the most fundamental way. Further, driving the need to prototype the case team element was the potential negative impact on the customer if the case team did not function as advertised.

With the scope and scale decision made the next challenge was determining how to prototype. The team concluded that the most effective way to prototype was to develop and document scripts. These scripts captured the way the team envisioned the new design working. They tested the scripts with insiders currently performing pieces of the case worker role, and with a very limited and very understanding set of customers. By talking through the scripts they were able to identify design weaknesses. The example in figure 2 is the cover page of one such script. The full scripts range from 3-10 pages each.

Process name:	Customer Interface & Order Management
Sub-process name:	Order entry
Description:	Fulfillment of a special Kodak sales offer
Prototype purpose:	Learn how to handle fax, credit card orders, deal with small customer accounts, test the information system conceptual design
Prerequisites:	Expert system in place, telecommunications available
Issues/Concerns:	Cost of the expert system may be prohibitive

Figure 2. CI&OM LCGM Prototype Script: Cover Page

Identifying pilot area(s)

As a result of executing the prototype the team will possess sufficient understanding to finalize the information system design, the specific job responsibilities, the physical layout of the workplace and other details necessary for implementation. The team will also be able to assess the need for a pilot and if a pilot is needed, will be able to establish the proper scope and scale of the pilot to gain maximum insights with minimum risk.

There are two decisions to be made in this step of the methodology:

1. Do you need to pilot the new design?
2. If a pilot is needed, how do we select what to pilot?

Both decisions can be made using a similar set of criteria. The pros and cons relative to the first question are: Assuming you choose to pilot, determining what to prototype will build off the same thinking. If the prototype pointed out many opportunities (problems) can a majority of the problems be associated with one or two aspects of the design? If so, include those aspects in the pilot so those problems can be resolved. Schedule is also an issue in determining what to pilot. If the project is right on schedule and you want to keep it that way don't take on more in the prototype than will fit into the available time window. If people are uncertain about their ability to perform the process consider selecting the aspects of their work that cause the most concern.

Reasons you might pilot	Reasons you might not pilot
The prototype pointed out many opportunities	The prototype uncovered few concerns
The overall project is right on schedule	The overall project is two months late
The design can be broken into meaningful segments	The design is highly integrated
We're not sure people know their jobs yet	People are confident in their abilities

Figure 3. Pros and Cons of Conducting a Pilot Center

By this point in the process the BPR team will have tremendous ownership for the redesign. Executing the pilot becomes a time when the new design must begin to be handed off to the process performers. If your change management effort has been effective, these implementation teams will also feel some ownership. Nonetheless, the hand-off requires great care and effort on the part of the BPR team.

Lessons learned: new process design

1. The redesign must be driven by customer needs, not by the desire to implement a new information system.
2. Process redesign is a time to employ one or more of the many creative group process techniques.
3. In communicating to stakeholders clearly link the new design to the business strategy and describe how the design will meet the business objectives stated in the case for action.
4. Have customers involved in the review of the macro redesign captured in the redesign table.
5. Initially, document just enough detail to enable stakeholders to see what is different from the current state, and to picture how the new process might actually operate. Create additional level of detail only at the point in time that it is needed.
6. As the redesign is validated with stakeholders, expect previously unspoken hard constraints to surface. These constraints may be real and will require modification of the design. Or they may be a form of resistance to change. Carefully assess each new hard constraint using the sponsor and the steering committee to help determine the validity of the constraint.
7. As stakeholders push back on the redesign (If they don't, something is really wrong!) defend the new process design from the customer's point of view, not the BPR team's.

Business Transition

Business transition is the implementation of the new business system and the supporting infrastructure. It starts with the pilot implementation. Results of the pilot are used to refine the design. The next step is to roll out the refined design across the entire scope and scale. If a pilot is not performed the implementation teams must regularly evaluate progress and apply findings to the ongoing implementation.

The activities in this phase are:

- Building and/or modifying the infrastructure to support the new business processes.
- Creating a master implementation plan to guide the work and track progress.
- Implementing the process in a pilot setting.
- Forming implementation teams and rolling out the new design across the business.

Building and/or modifying the infrastructure

Depending on the project, infrastructure may include information systems, telecommunications, physical distribution, manufacturing facilities and the like. Each of these may be a project unto itself, with its own implementation team, governance structure and project plan. The role of the BPR team is to ensure that the work of each implementation team is consistent with the overall design. In addition, the BPR team can play a role in removing roadblocks and continuing to drive the change management process.

Creating the master implementation plan

"There is a time for thinking and a time for action, and the two shouldn't be confused. Plan so that when people who participate in the detailed change are on the right track, you'll know it. Plan only to the degree necessary to guide the participants toward the desired objective. Keep plans fluid enough to allow wide latitude, but firm enough to stay on target." Grossman's (1974) advice is perfect for a change as complex and far reaching as reengineering.

The master implementation plan guides each element of the roll out and brings together the work of the various implementation teams. The master plan addresses each element of the holistic wheel to ensure the project is implemented in a way that reflects the intent of the new design. The master plan should consider each of the following elements.

- *Business process roll-out* — This aspect of the plan sequences the roll-out in terms of the scope and scale. For example the CI&OM LCGM process may be fully implemented in the United States, followed one at a time by each site around the world.
- *Business benefit and validation* — This section of the plan identifies how the success of the implementation will be measured, tracked and tested against the original goals. It also describes how and when this information will be communicated back to the stakeholders.
- *Organizational structure* — Defines how and when the transition to the new organizational structure will occur.
- *Operational support* — Addresses the resources and procedures required to support the new business process. Includes the support of the information technology, telecommunications and the like. For example, planning for the installation and maintenance of a new telecommunications network required by the new design.
- *Recognition* — Addresses the implementation of new management systems for evaluation, compensation and recognition.
- *Stakeholder management* — Defines the events and interventions required in the ongoing approach for managing the change process with respect to key stakeholders.
- *Education* — Describes the key educational interventions needed to help the enterprise understand the need for and the benefits of the new design.

- *Training* — Identifies the training plan required to build individual capability. Includes planning the content and timing of the training materials, the instructors and the participants. This includes training in all skills needed to perform the new process.
- *Systems acquisition and development* — Describes how and when hardware, software and other information technology infra-structure will be put in place.

Implementing the pilot

A pilot is the first live test with real customers. This means taking the results of the prototype, upgrading the design and testing it under controlled conditions. To create the controlled conditions you may want to limit the customers in the pilot to those that have been involved previously. That experience does a couple things. First, it gives them insight that other customers would not have. Insight that will contribute to upgrading the process on the fly. Second, they might better understand and appreciate that the changes are being made for their benefit. As such, they are more likely to tolerate an imperfect process now, for the prospect of a much better process long term. If it is not practical to limit the customers involved in the pilot it may be appropriate to limit the scope of the pilot. That is, you may pick one or two sub-processes and pilot those. For example, the LCGM CI&OM pilot might test only the order taking process.

Forming implementation teams

Implementation teams are made up of people that will be performing and supporting the new process. Seeding implementation teams with people from the original BPR team can help to ensure consistency with the intended design. Depending on the complexity of the project there could be many implementation sub-teams. As the work is spread amongst many groups of people, managing the master implementation plan takes on a heightened level of importance.

Lessons learned: business transition

1. Be successful! That is to say select a pilot implementation where the odds are stacked in your favor. There will be many skeptics looking for a reason to say, "I told you so." Don't give them the opportunity.
2. If the key management stakeholders have been right behind the team in their support this is the time for them to get out in front and

lead. Prepare them for this challenge.
3. Focus on the new metrics. Help people understand how they will be measured with respect to the new process. Doing so helps people to see themselves in the new environment.
4. Celebrate your successes.

References
Grossman, Lee. 1974. *The Change Agent.* New York, N.Y.: AMACOM.

Change Management

This discussion of change management comes after the explanation of the reengineering process for one simple reason, so that you understand the significance of what you're trying to accomplish when you commission a reengineering project and therefore recognize the critical role of change management in the ultimate success of that effort. In terms of sequence, application of change management comes first — starting the day the decision is made to reengineer.

Your ability to lead and mange change will make or break your reengineering effort. That is a bold statement, but one that is consistent with Kodak's experience, and supported by a 1993 Price Waterhouse study, in which they found that over 60% of the companies that were unsuccessful with reengineering cited change management as the primary reason (*Industrial Engineering* 1993). While sponsors and BPR teams initially fret over their ability to creatively design new business processes that will be capable of meeting far reaching goals, they should really concern themselves with how they will get people to support and actively participate in the change. As Dr. Hammer is fond of saying, "The soft stuff is the hard stuff."

Concepts in change management

A few words of definition and theory before turning to the practical aspects of change management. First, change management really has two aspects: leading change and managing change. Managing change is about the world of objects. Words like funding, resources, tasks, plans, schedules and milestones fill the conversations of those responsible for managing change. Experience in strategic planning and project management are appropriate for change managers. Leading change is about the world of people. Words like vision, possibility, motivation, energy, commitment, knowledge, understanding, skills, behavior, and satisfaction fill the conversations of those leading change (Lamport 1993). Clearly, the experience and skills required to lead change are different from those needed to manage change. People with success implementing complex projects or leading organizations through the "white space" created by dramatic growth or traumatic loss are needed. Most organizations have a number of competent change managers; change leaders tend to be less plentiful.

There are also a many change models. Two, in particular, are useful in guiding the thinking of the BPR team. In his book, *Managing Transitions*, William Bridges (1991) narrows the definition of change by breaking it into two components. He uses the term change to describe the situational aspects: the new site, the new boss, the new team or the new policy. For the psychological process people go through to come to terms with the new situation, he uses the term transition. The interventions defined in your change management plan must deal with both the external changes and the internal transitions. To those definitions Bridges applies a model for thinking about change management. His model has three components:

ENDING - TRANSITION - BEGINNING

Perhaps the most important contribution this model makes from a reengineering perspective is the idea that all change begins with an ending, and that ending or loss must be dealt with before effective transition can start and a new beginning can take place.

A second model developed by Elizabeth Kubler-Ross is a five phase model:

DENIAL - ANGER - BARGAINING - SADNESS - ACCEPTANCE

In working with terminally ill patients Kubler-Ross found a predictable pattern of events. First the patient denies the illness. This denial may be expressed by getting second and third opinions, running test after test in hopes of a different outcome. In reengineering this is analogous to arguing that the competitor isn't really that good, or that the benchmark data doesn't apply or that the drop in sales is temporary and is only a reflection of the poor economy.

Once the patient gets beyond denial, anger usually follows. The patient may look for someone to blame for their condition or might proclaim, "Why me?" Reengineering can bring about the same response. Usually the anger will be directed at management in general and possibly to the reengineering sponsor in particular.

Thirdly, patients bargain with themselves, their doctor and/or their god. If your project survives after all the venting associated with the anger stage, a similar bargaining may occur. A form of bargaining that is common is for the organization's continuous improvement projects to take on renewed life. Projects that have been dormant or slow moving suddenly are ready for implementation. Perhaps people hope they can bargain their way out of fundamental, dramatic, radical change by making the current process perform a little better.

Realizing that bargaining has not changed the course of the illness the patient experiences sadness and at times depression. Some never make it out of depression and die in this state. Others with the personal will and proper support find acceptance. Some go on to raise their life to new heights by championing fund raising for a cure, working with others suffering hardships or doing things with their life that they had always promised themselves. The enterprise undergoing reengineering can have these same breakthroughs to new levels of commitment and action needed to make reengineering and ultimately the organization a success.

The Kubler-Ross model is applicable to change brought about by reengineering because the emotions of the terminally ill patient tend to be similar to the emotions of the terminally ill organization. However, unlike the terminally ill patient the terminally ill organization has a choice; reengineer and survive or fade away.

An approach to leading and managing change
It should be clear by now that reengineering is about change. Not change for the sake of change, but change for dramatic improvement in customer-driven results. Such dramatic improvement requires radical redesign, and radical redesign means people are affected. To be successful change must be carefully orchestrated and administered. In the proper doses an organization can be invigorated and transformed, while an overdose can cause many unpleasant side effects. Fortunately there is a body of knowledge and a set of associated techniques devoted to the people side of change. Properly understood these concepts and techniques can be applied to obtain

just the right effect. These concepts and techniques cover four broad areas; human resource policy and practice, communications, organization development and education and training.

Why must we focus so hard on leading and managing change to be successful? One possibility is that like many companies with a technological heritage, Kodak has outstanding people with education and training in engineering and the sciences. For many of these individuals the natural tendency is to focus on the technical aspects of change: the information systems, the manufacturing facilities or the logistics capabilities. Easily overlooked are the people oriented dimensions of the change: redesigning attitudes, beliefs, behaviors and ultimately culture. This one-sided focus can prevent people issues from surfacing until a problem turns into a crisis. This natural tendency toward the technological changes and away from the people issues is compounded by the fact that some of these people are paralyzed due to their lack of knowledge, skills and especially experience to deal with the issues. To overcome this tendency the reengineering team must, at a minimum do three things:

1. Make sure you have a change agent on the team. The change agent is anyone inside or outside the organization who tries to affect change. Often the practitioner is uniquely positioned to play this role. The change agent may be a professional, educated in the field of behavioral science. Or, more often an insider experienced in creating change. Industrial engineers who developed their change agent skills in the factory and more recently in the white collar environment can become excellent change agents. Systems analysts can also be effective reengineering change agents because their work generally demands a process oriented approach. With the appropriate training human resource professionals can also be effective change agents because of their orientation toward people related issues. Management consultant's experience in dealing with change at high levels of the organization can provide them the background to become effective reengineering change agents. And, of course, supervisors and managers can be the ultimate change agent if they have the change skills to go along with direct authority to implement change. The change agent can be a full time team member, or can work with the team in a consulting mode (Bennis 1985).

2. Provide change management training for the reengineering team. There are two objectives for the training. The first is to help the team develop a personal understanding for what it means to experience a change. This type of experiential learning can create empathy and result in a change plan that drives change at the appropriate pace. The second objective is to provide the team with techniques so that they are able to help others understand, accept and eventually become supportive of the change.
3. Create a change management plan very early in the project life cycle and follow it with great discipline throughout. It has practically become cliché to talk about the rapid pace of change in the world and in the workplace. More than 20 years ago Alvin Toffler wrote that millions of psychologically normal people will experience an abrupt collision with the future when they fall victim to tomorrow's most menacing malady — the disease of change (Toffler 1971). Most would agree that the pace of change and the sweeping nature of the changes is even more dramatic and fundamental today than it was at the time of Toffler's writing. The reengineering change could become just another of the many changes already overwhelming your people. To prevent an overload the change must be led and managed in an intelligent way, with a plan to guide the effort. As the framework at a glance depicts, the change plan should start with communication of the business strategy and carry throughout the business transition phase.

Understanding stakeholders

With the dramatic changes inherent to reengineering, stakeholder resistance must be anticipated and plans but in place to work with that resistance. The change management plan begins with a clear understanding of the key stakeholders. It is useful to think of stakeholders in three broad categories: sponsors, agents and targets. Sponsors and agents have been described previously. Targets are those people that are affected in some way by the change.

Whether a sponsor, an agent or a target there are only two camps with respect to the change: advocates — those supporting the change, and resistors — those denying the need to change, speaking negatively about the change or just sitting on the sidelines. For those stakeholders that resist, identifying the source of their resistance provides the basis for designing the intervention. Hammer suggests there are four basic reasons that people resist change (Hammer 1992).

1. *Rationality* — Objectively the rational resister can see why this change is not good for them personally or for their organization. They may view it as a threat to their job security, status, existing relationships, career path or autonomy. The rational resister may demonstrate resistance by denying that a problem is severe enough to require such drastic change, or by arguing that the proposed solution won't be effective. Dealing with the rational resister requires intervention that points out the positive aspects of the change for the individual, while recognizing the resulting loss the change may cause. If that does not work and the person is someone that the enterprise would prefer to keep, incentives for supporting the change and disincentives for resisting should be established.

2. *Fear* — The fearful resister has uncertainty or anxiety about the change. They may be fearful that they will not be able to perform at the same level of excellence in the new business system. Often this fear and anxiety can lead people to assume the worst about what might happen to them. Fearful resisters are likely to demonstrate their resistance by denying the need for drastic change. They may also describe how busy they already are, and that they could not possibly find time to be involved in reengineering. To alleviate fear bread by uncertainty, create more certainty. That can be done by sharing information all along the way, at times in more detail than may seem necessary to the BPR team. Another positive tactic is to begin to educate and train to develop capability in the new process.

3. *Discomfort* — The resister doesn't feel right about the change. They may believe the change is in opposition to a long held belief about how things ought to be. Or they may see the change requiring them to behave in a way that is inconsistent with their own self image. These people will probably not openly resist. Instead they might demonstrate their resistance by continuing as if nothing is happening. To deal with this type of resister the change agents must continually reinforce the absolute necessity of the change, via the case for action. Because this person is resisting from emotion and not necessarily through logic it is

important to demonstrate empathy and concern by listening to their concerns. It can also be helpful to create communications and experiences that allow this type of resister to personally experience the future. This can be by involving them in the prototype or visiting another company that has implemented aspects of your new design.

4. *Skepticism* — Perhaps the most destructive type of resister is the skeptic. Skeptics either do not believe that anything will really change, or do not trust that the people creating the change are looking after their best interest. The skeptic will openly resist often by bringing up past failures of the organization in implementing large changes. Phrases like, "In theory that sounds good, but I know it can't work because..." or "We tried something just like this 10 years ago and we ended up worse off," are to be expected from the skeptic. The truly destructive skeptic may even go so far as to actively sabotage the effort. The most difficult part for reengineering change agents is that the skeptics are often right! That is, they are accurately stating the outcomes of previous failures. To combat this, the intervention with skeptics must demonstrate overwhelming commitment. The communication must be consistent. And, the team must demonstrate small successes by taking advantage of quick hits. Because skeptics can be so destructive, as a final resort the leadership may be forced to move the skeptics to a place in the organization where they will be out of the way, or escort them to the door.

It should not be assumed that all resistance is bad and must be eliminated. In fact, resistance can be educational and result in an improved design and implementation plan. It often comes from the very people that are truly concerned about the future of their business and want to be active in ensuring that the changes reengineering brings will be effective. It is also a sign that you really are doing something different. Imagine if your case for action or new process design brought no response from stakeholders. One would have to assume that the room was full of silent resisters, or more likely that they perceived no change.

To ensure that each key stakeholder is dealt with appropriately it is desirable to establish a one-to-one relationship between a BPR advocate (e.g. team member, sponsor, team leader, process owner) and each key stakeholder. This simple, but powerful technique starts with the assessment of the each key stakeholder relative to the change, and continues throughout the project with ongoing communication and involvement, as appropriate. The BPR advocate is responsible for tailoring and executing the intervention. The results of each intervention are fed back to the BPR team. Initially, each team member may have 2-4 stakeholders. As the project evolves this may grow to as many as 10 or more stakeholders, and require 50 percent of the team's time and effort.

There are a variety of assessment tools that can be used to understand the position of stakeholders and entire organizations:

- Historical audits to uncover past successes and failures to large scale change;
- Cultural audits to pinpoint potential barriers; and
- Situational audits to understand the current mind-set of the organization.

While the results of the audits can sometimes be revealing, perhaps the greatest value of the assessment process is that it actually starts the change process in motion. Simply facing the difficult questions that they pose can cause stakeholders to begin to think about the need for change.

It bears repeating that leading and managing change starts the moment the idea for reengineering is expressed right through implementation. Planning for a process that can take one year or more, where environmental changes are sure to happen along the way, can seem overwhelming and even wasteful. Therefore, the planning should occur by phase. That is, as each of the four phases of the methodology approach, the team should identify what intervention will occur with which stakeholders. The plan should be updated regularly and should reflect a rolling horizon of 1-3 months. In building and updating your change management plan for each phase consider how you will utilize each of these five elements.

1. *Communication* —As much as anything change is about communication. The biggest problem reengineering teams have with communication is the illusion that it has been effective. To be effective, communication must speak to the interests of the receiver, must provide for two way interchange, should occur with sufficient frequency and be delivered via a medium that is easily accessible to the target audience. Communication must

also be blatantly truthful, which at times will seem harsh. Communication must also be well timed and be delivered in a consistent manner. Since communication will be delivered by many different people in many different ways, it is essential to create communication packages. These packages, created by the team and updated frequently, will increase the likelihood that each message is similar. Lastly, the communications effort must be persistent. Do not assume that if a message was delivered once that it has been received even if it has been heard. In his book *Control Your Destiny or Someone Else Will,* Tichy (1993) writes that Jack Welch, the CEO of General Electric communicated the same basic message for more than five years at every possible opportunity before he began to sense that the message was being received. Welch recognized that it took people at least twice just to understand his vision: the third, fourth and fifth times for the skeptics to realize he was serious; and to finally embrace it. That's persistence.

2. *Leadership* —The executive sponsor, process champion, steering committee and team leader will play a major role in driving change. Consider the leadership strengths of each and define a role that takes advantage of those strengths. At a minimum these leaders must mobilize the necessary resources and set the direction by providing the objectives and vision. If they have the experience and charisma to motivate and inspire, even better. One simple technique is to look for small, symbolic acts to support the words. These acts can be designed to demonstrate the leader's personal commitment to the BPR work.

3. *Reinforcement*— Consider the existing rewards and recognition systems. Do they encourage behaviors that will maintain the status quo? If so, how can they be modified to reward people for embracing and even driving change to the new process? Formal performance evaluation and compensation systems are the most obvious, and will need to be redesigned to support the new business process, but reinforcers must exist during the transition. These systems may be informal and will probably be temporary. They are also necessary to begin to change what people think, say and do with respect to the reengineering project.

4. *Education and training*— It is easy to associate change management efforts with motivation. But for people to change, they must not only have the desire, but also the capability to change.

Depending on the individual, internal motivation or external reinforcers can provide the desire; education and training can provide the capability. During project initiation, this education and training should focus on the change process itself. Its aim should be to help people understand their own thoughts and emotions which may help them cope with, and eventually embrace the change. As the project progresses to new process design, the training may focus on building the personal capabilities required to enact the new process. For example, the new CI&OM LCGM design requires a case team approach rather than a functional specialist approach. This case team will require a much broader set of skills for those performing the new process. An extensive training plan, both classroom and on the job, was designed to develop those skills.

5. *Involvement* — A powerful and proven change technique is to involve people as much as possible in the design and execution of that change. The literature is full of success stories brought about by involving the people doing the work in the design of the work. The change management strategy must balance this involvement with schedule and funding limitations. At a minimum the team should plan for involvement of management level stakeholders during project initiation, key customers during process understanding and the people that will be enacting the process during business transition.

To support the stakeholder assessment and planning, this simple form is helpful (see figure 1).

Date:
Part 1: Assessment
Name of individual or group:
Category of stakeholder: Sponsor Agent Target   (pick one)
Current camp: Advocate Resister   (pick one)
Form of resistance: Rationality Fear Discomfort Skepticism (pick one)

Part 2: Plan

Techniques	Who	Will do what	By when
Communications			
Leadership			
Reinforcement			
Education & Training			
Involvement			

Figure 1. Stakeholder Assessment and Planning Form

Lessons learned: change management

1. Reengineering is about business processes, but it is even more about people. Understand the politics and personalities involved and develop a change management plan to help people overcome their own barriers to change.
2. The change management process can consume up to 50 percent of the BPR team's time. This can be controlled to some degree, but at a minimum the change management plan must address how key stakeholders will be educated and updated.
3. If resistance isn't obvious in some form, either it is hidden or you're not really reengineering.
4. Do not wait for resistance to surface. Anticipate it and have a plan to diffuse it.
5. Leading and managing change is difficult and requires consistency and persistence on the part of all reengineering change agents.
6. All the evidence suggests that it is impossible to over communicate.

References

Bennis, Warren G. 1985. *The Planning of Change, Fourth Edition.* Cambridge, Mass.: Harvard Business College.

Bridges, William. 1991. *Managing Transitions: Making the Most of Change.* Reading, Mass.: Addison-Wesley.

Hammer, Michael. 1992. Seminar-*Reengineering: The Implementation Perspective.* Cambridge, Mass.: Center for Reengineering Leadership.

Institute of Industrial Engineers. 1993. Companies applying reengineering worried about managing change. *Industrial Engineering.* Norcross, Ga.: June.

Lamport, Ken. 1993. *Leading and Managing Change.* Kodak Imaging Organizational Development.

Tichy, Noel. 1993. *Control Your Destiny or Someone Else Will: How Jack Welch is Turning GE into the World's Most Competitive Corporation.* New York, N.Y.: Doubleday.

Toffler, Alvin. 1971. *Future Shock.* New York, N.Y.: Bantam.

Reengineering Lessons Learned at Kodak

In his classes, seminars, books and articles, Dr. Hammer relates lessons he has learned through his experiences with many enterprises attempting to reengineer. He does this to help newcomers avoid time consuming or even fatal mistakes. Despite Hammer's best efforts there are still some things that everyone seems to need to experience to learn. These are some of the lessons Kodak learned the hard way. Perhaps by embracing these you can avoid the errors of your predecessors.

- Lack of strong leadership will kill a reengineering project. Maybe not right away, but slowly, painfully.
- Incrementalism in the design process will lead to a result that is probably better than the current state but inadequate to meet the objectives stated in the case for action. To avoid incrementalism do not start with what exists, but rather with a clean sheet.
- Inadequate attention to the people side of reengineering will undermine the most elegant redesign. This lesson is hard to grasp because there are so many ways to go wrong (e.g., starting too late, stopping too soon, insufficient frequency, inconsistency, inappropriate timing, one way communication vehicles that don't allow for feedback, etc).
- Not uncovering design constraints until the new design is ready for implementation. Constraints that are uncovered early can be dealt with, constraints that show up late can be catastrophic.

- Focusing on the new information system, the boss or the internal politics, instead of focusing on the only stakeholder group that, in the end really matters — the customer.

Fortunately not all the things Kodak has learned were through failure. We have also learned some things about what works by doing them very well.

- Understand the customer's business by spending time with them on their turf.
- Create a positive BPR team environment by co-locating the team and providing freedom from the usual bureaucracy inherent in the culture of a large corporation.
- Move quickly through the process. Do not be afraid of missing something because whether you go slow or fast you will miss something. Expect and anticipate that new information and understanding will arise and be prepared to continually up-grade as the team learns and grows.
- Design business processes that focus on making the interaction with your company simple, fast and even enjoyable.

Part Two

Case Studies in Development and Implementation of BPR

A
Case Study
by
Connie Brittain

BellSouth

In 1991, Atlanta-based BellSouth lost approximately $1.3 billion in net revenue to competitors — nearly the same amount as the company's net income. Those who believe that the company is too big, too tough to falter, need to notice the experiences of such firms as IBM, General Motors, Sears and Pan Am to name a few.

Competitors are not waiting for BellSouth to wake up. Once content to nibble the edges, they are now taking bigger bites from the company's business.

For instance, one of the nation's largest banks in Atlanta turned to Metropolitan Fiber Systems (MFS) for access to its long-distance carrier — because MFS's bid was less than one-third that of Southern Bell, the local telephone company owned by BellSouth.

In Louisville, Ky., the local school district chose a branch of Cincinnati Bell — rather than BellSouth's South Central Bell — to supply its voice messaging system. Historically, Cincinnati Bell did not operate in BellSouth's territory — but the company saw an opportunity and acted on it.

In Orlando, Fla., one of the nation's largest media and cable companies, Time Warner Inc., announced plans to build an interactive, two-way "electronic super highway." According to the *Wall Street Journal,* the system will be designed "to deliver movies on demand, interactive games, home shopping and telephone services." Time Warner is now certified as an alternate access provider by the Florida Public Service Commission. This means the company can now directly compete with BellSouth for special access and private-line service. A similar request has been made for Tennessee.

There are more than 250 fiber installations in BellSouth's nine-state region that belong to other organizations. These include power companies, cable companies, government agencies, medical firms, universities and competitive access providers. As many as 13,000 other locations — stores, banks, offices and other sites — are linked by small, privately operated satellite dishes.

Plus, consider the competition in other forms — cable and newspaper companies, other telephone companies, long-distance companies. Consider the implications of AT&T's planned investment in McCaw Communications Cellular. In 1983, AT&T was the mother company for all the regional Bell operating companies. Today, it wants to buy a controlling interest in McCaw Cellular and become part owner of one of the nation's largest cellular network operators and a leading advocate of a nationwide wireless network. If AT&T and McCaw develop such a wireless network, they could easily bypass local telephone companies to provide long-distance or local calling networks. It is not impossible that the Bell holding companies, restricted by government regulations, could be left behind — the way railroads were left behind when the automobile appeared.

From Australia to Atlanta, Ga., BellSouth has built a strong presence in markets, from cellular, paging, and directory advertising and publishing to advanced communications applications. But nothing comes easy in a world where everyone wants a piece of the pie. It is time for a reality check. The pace and turbulence in the modern business world has been compared to "permanent whitewater."

The competitive waters around BellSouth are rising so fast that the corporation must virtually "re-invent" itself for the 1990s. Consider:

- Some 10,000 jobs have been eliminated from the operations since 1990 and at least 8,000 more will be gone by 1996.
- In 1991, the staffs of BellSouth Enterprises and BellSouth Corp. began merging. And BellSouth Services, South Central Bell and Southern Bell were "recombined" to form BellSouth Telecommunications (BST).

BST, with headquarters in Atlanta and Birmingham, Al., provides unified direction and support for the local telecommunications operations of BellSouth in the southeastern U.S. and for the operations of Dataserv Inc., BellSouth Communications Inc., and BellSouth Communications Systems Inc. BST conducts business under the name of Southern Bell in North Carolina, South Carolina, Georgia and Florida; and South Central Bell in Kentucky, Tennessee, Alabama, Mississippi and Louisiana.

BST's combined operations serve more than 18.6 million local telephone lines and provide local exchange and intraLATA long-distance service over one of the most modern telecommunications networks in the world. Leaders in optical fiber deployment, Southern Bell and South Central Bell have more than 900,000 miles in their network. BST employs 82,866 employees who are organized into four primary groups: marketing, network and technology, regulatory and external affairs, and services.

At BST, there is a growing focus on fundamentally new ways of getting jobs done. Business process reengineering (BPR) along with the Total Quality System will help reshape BST's way of doing business for the future.

"We're in the first stage of a long process — a process that's absolutely necessary for our future success. And one that will radically change BellSouth Telecommunications, just as our business environment has changed dramatically," says Duane Ackerman, BST president and CEO.

The biggest issue facing companies is organizational inflexibility with regard to accepting change, says BST assistant vice president/reengineering Dennis Strickland. The momentum for most companies is for the status quo, which is organizational inertia, he says. "I get hundreds of questions fired at me, such as, 'Are you sure we can do this?' 'Are we moving too fast?' 'What about the labor relations issues?' The questions are all negative. No one asks, 'Is that all we can do?' 'Can we do it faster?' 'Can't we get greater improvement?' Overcoming the human resistance to change is the biggest single issue in reengineering," Strickland says.

Change means cutting costs and building corporate structures to give customers what they want, how and when they want it, and at a competitive price. Three interrelated factors occur when change for the better takes place:

- an increased focus on customers and quality;
- the introduction of new technologies; and
- a competitive edge due to a reduction of costs.

The decision to reengineer
Over the last six to eight years the company has made force reductions

through such methods as early outs, normal attrition, etc. "However, we realized that if we were to continue to cut costs and improve service, we were going to have to shoot more accurately with a rifle rather than a shotgun," says Strickland. "We decided we needed to be more specific, remove work content and get those people out as opposed to trying to get a cross section of people off the payroll and experience the back fill and churn that comes with it, and then try and put people in the right jobs," he says.

Initially, the company's primary motivation to consider reengineering was because of downsizing and the need to be aware the market is changing, the work content is changing and the market demands are changing. Reengineering is also about improving customer satisfaction, positioning the company for increased revenue and saving money on non-labor costs, such as net bad debt recovery and inventories. One of the values of reengineering is the ability to go in with an interdepartmental force and take a look at a specific business process all at once. Then describe it in detail, looking at every task that takes place from start-to-finish, along with the data and reports used to support each task, and try to make a giant leap as opposed to chipping away at it. In the process, certain questions need to be asked:

- What is really trying to be accomplished?
- Why is something being done the way it is?
- How could something be done if it were starting from scratch?

BST initially addressed eighty-one processes and used some 300 employees to begin the reengineering effort. Some reengineering efforts were accomplished without a consultant — centralizing BST's data processing centers for instance. However, ultimately the company realized assistance was needed. So in early to mid 1991, BellSouth invited several reengineering consultants to make presentations. United Research was selected, which has since changed its name to Gemini as a result of a merger. The firm continues to work with the BST reengineering effort. Gemini brought objectivity and a disciplined process that enabled BST to look at the facts and not just try to answer questions the way insiders thought they should be answered. That helps with the maverick, out-of-box thinking required for successful reengineering efforts. Gemini also helped handle confrontational issues.

Gemini's process is called a brown paper process. The firm

spent eight to 12 weeks performing various kinds of analyses on how BST's operation worked and then put it on a huge brown paper, like wrapping paper on a big roll. It was then rolled out along a wall to visualize how the whole process works. The recommendation was to divide BST's business into 12-13 different processes to improve costs, customer satisfaction and revenue strength.

BST did not start immediately on all 12-13 processes. Over the months these processes have changed. "We are not looking at the whole business from end to end, but the 12-13 most important parts," says Strickland. "We call these process streams," he says. "Reengineering looks at process streams across an organization instead of seeing it functionally or geographically. If you look broadly across what the input, processes, function and output are, then you can have wider latitude on what to change," he says. "The number of areas can change as priorities change. Reengineering pulls together related functions as early in the process as possible, rather than after they are completed. Reengineering arranges for those who use the output of the process to be the ones who perform it. And reengineering organizes toward outcomes rather than around tasks, so that one person performs all of the related steps in the process. It puts the decision-making where the work is performed and captures information once — at its source — so that the unit that produces the information also processes it. In reengineering, you don't end up where you started," says Strickland.

Selecting the reengineering team

Different areas have different teams, which vary in size, from project to project, from process stream to process stream, and from time to time during the life of the project. There have been anywhere from 10 to 70 people involved on a team at a given time. Different skill sets and experiential backgrounds had to be considered. The work is intense and sometimes people cannot work for three years on a project, but work best for six to nine months or even a year and a half before needing to change.

BST looked for people with appropriate technical background and those who had the respect of the individuals they would be working with in analyzing the system. "The importance of that cannot be over-emphasized," Strickland says. People demonstrating ability as free thinkers were also sought.

Orientation and training encompassed three to five days spread out over three to four weeks. Those chosen were told what had been accomplished and what BST reengineering was about. They were then given materials to read and an opportunity to learn all pertinent terms. Horizon expanding exercises were also practiced to help get people thinking outside-of-the-box. Then there was team-work training to learn to depend on one another.

Problems encountered

Problems focused on two areas. The first area was the easier of the two — how to come up with a better solution. The harder problem encompassed putting the solution into doable terms. "Whenever you talk about cutting costs out of a company, it's threatening," says Strickland. "It could be your job or a friend's, or you might have to move or learn new skills. Those are all big concerns," he says. Those are morale and motivation concerns for the company. But the organizational inflexibility is an even bigger problem. Such big companies take on an institutionalism that makes change difficult. "Problems start at the top and flow down. So people higher in any business need to ask ourselves have we got our heads on straight and are we willing to make changes," says Strickland.

BST does a case analysis on everything to be done before any change that involves investment occurs. Essentially this is an eco-nomic analysis that lays out the costs, benefits and anticipated returns. Ackerman and the executive policy counsel, which includes the group presidents, look at change management in terms of what they are calling management agenda. This is to assure that everyone is looking at the basic issues in the business and enabling change, not inhibiting it.

"I recognize that a critical factor to reengineering's success is support from top management. That's why I'm personally involved in making sure our reengineering effort is working and working well. And I expect every key manager running BellSouth Telecommunica-tions to share this same commitment. If their support isn't in place, reengineering will not work," Ackerman says.

Resistance has been a big problem. "Everyone is resistant to change," says Strickland. "And reengineering is change — big time. It's big change, deep and quick. No one will say they are not for reengineering. It's like saying they are against apple pie and mother-hood," says Strickland. "People will even vote for the need to change something. But trouble arises when it's pointed out that they, too, will have to make some changes. There is particular resistance to some-one coming from the outside trying to tell you how you ought to change your operation," he continues.

An experience Strickland had just out of college some 25 years ago has helped him alter his thinking. After working for six months, Strickland went to his boss with what he believed was a great idea. Basically, the idea focused on getting another organization to change so Strickland could work better and get faster results. His boss responded that he wanted Strickland to spend all his time focusing on how he could change what he was doing because he could not control what others were doing. It's human nature to point at the other person. But that experience stuck with Strickland and today he always initially thinks, "What can I do differently?"

Reengineering versus total quality

Change management and cultural change are both needed for there to be dramatic change in the business like reengineering purports to do. "Changing corporate culture is one of the most demanding challenges any company faces because it takes time and requires far more than an edict from on high," says Becky Dunn, BST vice president/human resources and benefits administration. "Through emphasis on learning and incorporating the total quality process along with reengineering, people are beginning to shift their viewpoint and adopt new ideas," says Dunn. "Also, more is being done via employee information to communicate the competitive and financial realities of the industry. There are published hot line phone numbers employees can call to learn more about reengineering plans and related human resources programs and how they will affect them."

Changes are occurring in the ways employee performance is evaluated, how salaries for various jobs are determined, and decisions on individual salary increases. Leadership feedback has also been introduced. On a yearly basis, management asks their people through a questionnaire," How am I doing?" The new programs stress the importance of setting difficult-to-reach goals, says Dunn. Because it is also important for the company itself to demonstrate its willingness to change, new work options such as job-sharing and telecommunications are being tried out. Other programs available include: sabbatical leave; transitional leave, a career continuation program; training; a supplemental income protection plan; an expanded supplemental income protection plan; and a voluntary protection program.

Reengineering and total quality have aspects in common:

- Both are based upon the premise that superiority in business

process performance is critical to competitiveness.
- Both require that senior management lead and manage extensive organizational change.
- Both require teams of people to implement new procedures and programs.
- Both improve relationships between customers and suppliers, empower employees and improve products and processes.

The biggest single difference between total quality and reengineering is that reengineering is a one-time effort. It looks at the major parts of the company in a very detailed and organized way and identifies areas in which to streamline the processes that involve multiple departments. Quality, on the other hand, is a never-ending quest.

Actually, at BST, the quality effort preceded the reengineering effort. Says Strickland, "The quality effort is much more pervasive. We're trying to get people to think and reflect quality in all their decisions. Through the quality process we are trying to infuse the discipline to maintain continuous improvement so we can reengineer a process that is already being run in a quality manner and make another large leap and continue to improve it through quality application principles."

BST and other BellSouth companies determined that in the U.S. the Malcolm Baldrige Quality Award criteria is the best description of what a quality company should be. Considering it to be a strong management model, BST is using it to access the degree of accomplishment in quality deployment and to integrate quality into all BST business functions and processes so it becomes automatic.

Quality is a very precise, disciplined way of managing a business. But it takes time to achieve integration. And patience is not a quality valued in many companies that are action-oriented. People at BST are learning aggressive patience.

Hal Davis, BST director/corporate quality, describes how quality and reengineering integrate. "If a line were drawn with continuous improvement written at the left end and reengineering written at the right end, the two represent a continuum for improving and changing business processes. At the far end and up to about 30 percent of the line represents the total quality system. We look at all of the processes in the business and seek opportunities to improve the efficiency and effectiveness of those processes," says Davis. "We encourage individuals and natural teams that work together in the business to continuously look at the daily work that they do and question what they do and what they get as input to the process that they are working in, what they do with it, and what they provide to their customers, whether internal or external," says Davis. "In reality, a good product needs to result and value needs to be added.

"At the 30 percent point and beyond there are increasing complexities of processes on which to seek continuous improvement. The methods used correspondingly increase in sophistication regarding the tools used to study, measure and fix a process. At the 30 percent point and beyond you get into the ranks of reengineering," says Davis. Davis describes reengineering as the revolution of work processes, turning them upside down, looking for ways to radically change the way we have done business or are doing business presently. "We are no longer interested in making subtle improvements to the processes but are looking for radical change that would cause significant efficiencies in those processes," he adds.

Reengineering and quality complement one another. Says Davis, "Once you finish reengineering a process, the first thing you do is look for ways to improve it. So you use your quality principles." Measurement is common to both applications and is a key for achieving success. "There is a dearth of good measurers in any company to help evaluate how you're doing," says Davis. "The ability to look at what we're doing now, quantify that activity, and then change it, and then quantify it again is the basis for showing improvement, whether from reengineering or from a total quality system," he says.

Most companies today recognize that in a competitive global economy, cost will play a preeminent role in the ability to compete in the future. BST's reengineering effort attempts to identify those processes that can be changed as well as efficiencies that can be gained to allow the company to reach its cost objectives. By 1996, 8,000 jobs will be eliminated. There needs to be a realization of the anticipated effects of downsizing on a company's operations prior to downsizing occurring. And if jobs are eliminated and work content is not, then the reengineering effort has failed.

Forecasting and budgeting

Forecasting and budgeting and service activation were the first two reengineering processes focused upon. Forecasting and budgeting focuses on the design and development of new budget and forecasting processes to link strategies, plans and budgets to ensure the best use of resources to achieve corporate goals. However, the budgeting term used is really a misnomer. It really means improving business allocation procedures. Improvement was needed to make certain the company was matching expenditure of resources to strategic directions. Commissioned January 1992, a joint task force studied 81 distinct processes, interviewing more than 260 employees. There was room for improvement in communications between departments and the planning organizations. The entire process was studied without regard to departmental lines. It was found that the company can make significant improvements in effectiveness through streamlining work and through additional mechanization. Areas being addressed include: business planning, business inventory, financial analysis and strategic resource allocation. The budgeting and resource allocation process, called SMART, which includes expense, capital and revenue budgets, has been implemented.

Forecasting is responsible for providing growth projections used by network, marketing and other departments. The study of the forecasting organization focused on process flows and streamlining opportunities. It was found that the company can make significant improvements in effectiveness through streamlining work and through additional mechanization. Consolidations at state headquarters locations will take place in all nine states, resulting in approximately 150 jobs being phased out.

Complex Business ESSX® is a relatively small, narrowly focused reengineering project that will simplify processes of selling, ordering and implementing ESSX service, and seek to simplify design of the product. ESSX is a central office-based service. BST has automated by putting in a front-end system to all the down-stream service activation processes in just the ESSX service. So instead of filling out a long, manual form, making 14 photocopies, and mailing it to 100 people, it was typed into a computer and people get what they need.

The Comptrollers-Core (comptrollers optimizing resource effectiveness) project will identify work-process changes to simplify work, consolidate functions and improve cost-effectiveness. The most significant change is that most comptroller operations will be consolidated in a few locations rather than being performed in all nine states. For instance, revenue accounting will be consolidated in Birmingham; there will be two message investigation centers — in Columbia, S.C. and Birmingham; and bills will be mailed from five locations — Birmingham, Charlotte, N.C.; Jackson, Miss.; Nashville, Tenn.; and

Miami, Fla. Plus, mail remittance operations will have three locations — Charlotte; New Orleans, La.; and Atlanta. And there will be one property and cost accounting center — in Atlanta. Certain functions will continue to be performed in each state. These include enhanced billing services and state billing coordination. Outside plant property records will remain in each state except South Carolina.

Data center consolidation is the new strategy for reducing the number of data centers from 20 to six and creating a test/development center. This project is ongoing through the fourth quarter of 1994.

Service activation

Begun in October 1991, Service Activation is one of BST's older, core streams. It will examine the entire process from order initiation to service installation, enhancing customer satisfaction and improving cost-effectiveness.

To the customer, placing an order for service and getting it installed looks simple, but behind the scenes is a labyrinth of processes built up over decades. Because of that complexity, the way a service order is activated was a natural early project for BST's reengineering effort. To get a good picture of how the service order flow works now, two sites were picked — Louisville and Fort Lauderdale, Fla. Four weeks were spent at each location observing and talking with the people there about what and how things were being done.

One of the first things noticed was that the service rep gives the customer a commitment date for installation, but the work is not assigned until further down the line. That can lead to problems. For example, if the order requires a site visit but the service reps do not know it, the order may take longer than the customer is told it will take. One planned change will result in the work being assigned immediately. The service rep, seeing the assignment information on the computer screen, can tell the customer with more confidence when the service will be installed.

Five initiatives for this project include:

- introducing a new terminal emulation system in the recent change memory administration centers across the region;
- computerizing the error resolution process and enhancing the service order delivery systems to reduce the number of errors in the residence and business service centers;
- automating the testing, analysis and tracking of service orders

that require dispatch;
• using a single platform for address maintenance and database synchronization; and
• enhancing software and procedures that track the assignment of telephone numbers.

Most of the early efficiency gains will come from eliminating redundant processes. In error correction, one project already completed, allows service representatives to call up records with incorrect data on a computer screen. Under the old process, they had to sift through printouts, many of which listed errors that had already been caught and corrected.

The team set out to design the system it would create if unrestricted by budgets, existing systems or internal politics. Projects were broken into those that could be done within six months, those that could be done within 18 months and long-term projects that would require more than 18 months. BST is at the stage of building a bridge from the old environment to the new one. Completion is expected by the end of 1994.

Other key areas
Central office operations, another core stream, has some 40 people focusing on redesigning central office related processes. Equal emphasis will be given to internal central office operations and those that affect other business functions. It is ongoing through the fourth quarter 1995. It merged with the repair maintenance process, another core stream, which reviews, redesigns and improves processes related to repair and maintenance. Some 40 people work on this project too, which is to be ongoing through the third quarter 1994. The two projects focus on BST's core product provided: the telephone service and maintenance.

Information technology takes a complete look at all information resources in BST in order to align them with corporate strategies and priorities in the most effective manner. It covers BST information systems, user management group and staff support organizations.

Network planning and provisioning is still another BST core stream. It seeks to reduce expenses related to the planning and provisioning process, improve work-order cycle time, eliminate re-work, improve quality and ensure effective deployment of capital investments. It constitutes more than half BST's workforce — 41,000 employees. This project began fourth quarter 1992 and should be completed around second quarter 1995.

Organizational alignment will align structure, systems, human resources and accountabilities of BST to best support reengineered business processes and strategic direction. This was begun fourth quarter 1993 and should be completed first quarter 1996.

Business office revenue recovery will focus on business processes related to collections, seeking improvements in margin performance and cost of capital. This will begin first quarter 1994 and be completed first quarter 1996.

Business office sales and service excellence, also called overall efficiency, will examine business office operations with emphasis on improving customer contact and handling of service order errors. There are not a large number of functions in this project but it represents a fairly big and significant piece of BST business. This will begin second quarter 1994 and be completed first quarter 1996.

Regulatory will examine business process such as rate development and filing processes, along with definition of roles and responsibilities and alignment with BST business strategy. It too, will begin second quarter 1994 and be completed first quarter 1996. "My desire is to run reengineering where it has a beginning, a middle and an end," says Strickland. "We have a product process that we can rely on. We do have a regular organization though it may be changed when we get through with this," he says. "A company needs to run the regular business day to day without having a group of people on the side lines trying to make large scale change. That's not to say that as the business changes and the market changes that there might not be future needs to do something like reengineering. But by that time it will probably have a different name, a new buzz word. So reengineering, like everything else, has a life span.

"I don't think reengineering allows you to accomplish any one specific strategy. It complements you in all your major strategies," says Strickland.

"We are learning about flexibility in the workplace," adds Davis. "Flexibility and speed are the keys to any company's success in the future."

A
Case Study
by
Brad Bambarger

Carrier Transicold

Even as it seemed to most that Carrier Transicold (CTD) was on the right road — with a proud past and present of market leadership — some of its managers and engineers knew that the company would have to cast off tradition and learn new ways, regardless of the company's current favorable position, or much of its accomplishment would soon erode. For a sizable organization like CTD, major change is almost always difficult. But it's especially hard when the company appears to be at the top of its game. Overt, pressing problems tend to create a "foxhole" mentality that helps a company rally and implement change to ensure its survival. When the problems aren't so palpable, when there are merely hints of hardship on the horizon, trying to garner the commitment and competence for change can be daunting.

Motivated by these concerns for the future and inspired by the successful innovations of Japanese manufacturers, CTD is meeting the challenge of business process reengineering (BPR) by going back to school. That is, it is taking the basis of a newly designed manufacturing method — what is known as the Carrier Lean Production System (CLPS) — to the University of Tennessee (UT), where the company teams with faculty experts and graduate students to research and implement this new means of doing business.

CTD engineers, manufactures and services transport refrigeration and air-conditioning systems as a division of Carrier Corp., headquartered in Farmington, Conn. Established in 1915 by Dr. Willis H. Carrier — the inventor of modern air conditioning — Carrier became part of the United Technologies group of companies in 1979. (Also the parent company of Pratt & Whitney, Sikorsky Helicopters and others, United Technologies is the fifth largest manufacturer in the United States, with more than 170,000 employees and annual sales exceeding $22 billion.) Helping its customers meet stringent temperature control demands for such cargo as meat and dairy products, fruits and vegetables, blood plasma, flowers and film, CTD has put environmental control systems in everything from fishing boats to aircraft carriers, from trucking fleets to NASA's Apollo program. With almost 3,000 employees worldwide, CTD approaches $800 million in sales.

With that sort of corporate profile, you would think that CTD would turn to a Big Six consulting firm for assistance rather than look to a Southeastern Conference university in Knoxville, Tenn. Perhaps against the grain, CTD has had an ongoing relationship with UT since 1991, conducting research and training via the College of Business Administration's Management Development Center. The catalysts for this alliance have been Hume Laidman, CTD vice president of manufacturing, and Dr. Thomas Greenwood, assistant professor with the University (Ph.D. in industrial engineering and a senior member of IIE) and founder of The Lean Production Systems Design Institute. One of a number of quality and customer focus institutes that operate through the University's Management Development Center, the Lean Production Systems Design Institute has also had attendees to training programs from Allied-Signal, LTV Steel Co., IBM and The HON Co., among others. Its relationship with CTD, however, is especially close.

Greenwood has been helping CTD transform its business processes using lean production systems, or CLPS. Helping make CLPS an umbrella program for all CTD manufacturing facilities, he has trained and advised managers and engineers at each of the company's production sites (except for the new Singapore location). CTD's plants in Athens, Ga., Syracuse, Rouen, France, Mexico City, York, Pa., and Montreal are in varying stages of reengineering their operations, making use of CLPS research and training conducted with the University, as well as the school's graduate student interns.

Carrier Lean Production System

Prior to its reengineering efforts with CLPS, CTD's production facilities operated with traditional batch manufacturing processes. The plants were typical of many U.S. factories, with large in-process inventories, poorly defined process flow and a work force conditioned to narrow roles and responsibilities. With the refrigerated transport industry experiencing a real growth rate of approximately 10 percent a year, customer demand for higher quality and quicker delivery spurred CTD to move toward more modern, customer-responsive manufacturing strategies.

The reengineering of each CTD facility begins with an examination of its customers' needs, so that the motivating force behind its production — the rationale behind the work of each employee — becomes "delivering value to the customer." Though essential, product quality and speed-to-market for new products are not enough. CTD's formula for the future is to distinguish its offerings in the marketplace by anticipating customer needs and making the satisfaction of those needs flexible and timely.

In its CLPS program, CTD has two sets of goals — one strategic, the other tactical. Stemming from the company's mission of delivering value to its customers, the strategic, corporate goal of CLPS is "to increase the competitive position of [CTD's] products by instituting processes that are more effective, efficient, economical and responsive to market fluctuations," Laidman says. The tactical, or plant-by-plant, goals include: improving delivery lead times; reducing human effort in production and design; condensing manufacturing space; boosting manufacturing throughput; decreasing time-to-market for new products; lowering tooling costs; improving quality indices; and increasing total raw material, work-in-progress and finished-good inventory turns (annual dollar sales divided by average inventory dollars).

According to Greenwood, in reinventing its production processes to achieve these goals, each CTD facility relies on these principles of CLPS:

- Process-oriented management (through cross-functional management/engineering teams);
- Customer focus (gauging value via time, cost and quality);
- Teamwork and communication (emphasizing visual signals and instructional method sheets);
- Prudent use of resources (graduating from economies of scale to economies of scope);
- Elimination of waste (cutting nonvalue-added tasks, reducing overproduction and scrap); and
- Continuous improvement (pursuing the Japanese ideal of kaizen).

"CLPS combines the best aspects of both craft and mass production techniques, allowing CTD to design and produce a variety of products 'customized' to specific orders and delivered with slim lead times," Greenwood says. "To achieve these goals, CTD has had to develop flexible, short-cycle product design and manufacturing capabilities as well as responsive distribution channels. The company is also changing the way its products go to market, developing time-based marketing strategies and rate-based planning techniques to balance production and supplier capacities against variations in demand."

In CTD's new lean production environment, the overall product delivery process comprises five individual activities, as explained by Greenwood (see figure 1):

Flow manufacturing — "Usually the first, as well as the most visual, redesign activity in lean production implementations is to reduce manufacturing throughput times by creating flow manufacturing processes. Plants have to be converted from departmental factory layouts and batch processing to product-oriented manufacturing cells and one-piece processing. The volume and cycle time of

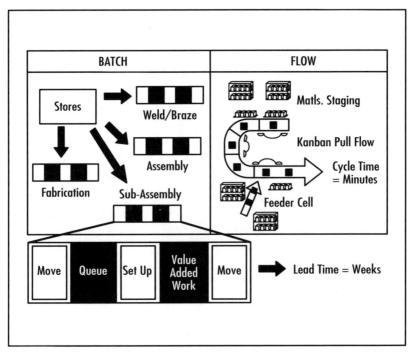

Figure 1. Batch vs Flow Manufacturing

products manufactured are set according to customer demands, and the production sequence is mixed to ensure smooth demand from both internal resources and external suppliers."

Rate-based production planning — "To cope with varying customer demands, a facility plans for an agreed-on level of flexibility regarding both quantity and model mix changes over time. Then, as the plant develops newer forecasts and receives actual orders, production levels are allowed to flex up or down in response to daily requirements — in accordance with upper and lower demand limits."

Rate-based order management — "To make sure that promised orders are compatible with capacity, sales and marketing must stay informed of day-by-day production boundaries and communicate with both customers and production to manage multiple order plans and time-based delivery mechanisms. One order management strategy would draw on a limited amount of stocked finished goods to provide immediate response for that group of customers wanting 'at-once' delivery. Another strategy would be to forward schedule the majority of demand requirements that are built-to-order and backward schedule planned orders that are promised beyond the current lead time. The idea is to manage an array of order plans, each tailored to a particular market segment and its timing needs. The eventual goal is to reduce lead times to the point where all demand is satisfied by building units to order."

Rate-based materials management — "To deliver on the commitments of rate-based planning and management, a plant has to establish new, more responsive supply lines. Longer term supplier relationships, joint development efforts and, most important, information sharing are crucial to lean production. To help ensure that quality materials are delivered in the right quantity, right mix and at the right time and place, a plant has to utilize all the tools at its disposal — including MRP [materials requirement planning] and EDI [electronic data interchange]. EDI, for instance, can be a 'paperless' means of continually, automatically updating suppliers on a plant's future materials needs." (See figure 2.)

Time-based distribution channels — "After the company anticipates the customers' needs and manufactures a value-added product, it still has to get the product into the customers' hands promptly or all that front-end effort is for naught. Frequent direct customer shipments are a prime option, and they can be made cost-effective by integrating distribution with the supply side of the production process. 'Milk runs' — or dedicated inbound and outbound transporta-

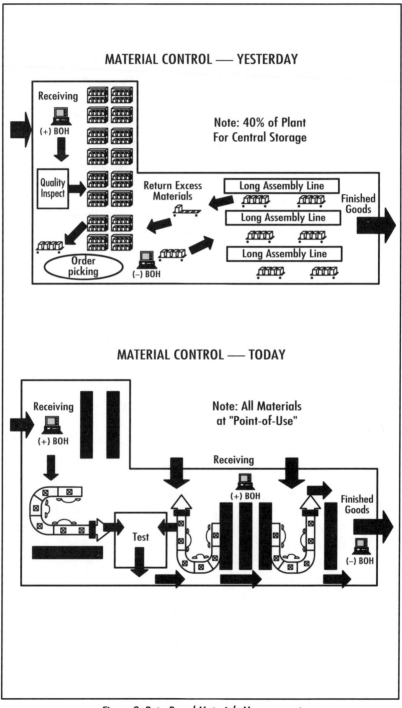

Figure 2. Rate-Based Materials Management

tion routes — can be developed that not only smooth deliveries but afford load quantity discounts from carriers."

CLPS on the line

A reference point for CTD's reengineering with CLPS has been the company's truck/trailer product operation in Athens, Ga. The CLPS program there was initiated by former plant manager Tim Cosgrove, who — through his facility's productivity gains — was instrumental in evoking enthusiasm among corporate officers for the immediate benefits and future potential of CLPS. Now CTD's director of manufacturing resources, Cosgrove passed the torch in 1993 to Jim Ferguson, the current Athens plant manager, who has continued BPR efforts at this major CTD facility, integrating CLPS with ISO 9000 certification. A primary accomplishment of CLPS thus far at Athens, Ferguson says, has been to reduce fabrication shortages. "We've eliminated lost time from shortages as much as 50 percent and increased throughput by 20 percent over 1992. Introducing kanbans has allowed us to reduce hassles and be more material-responsive without excess paperwork... In 1993, we increased our throughput by over 30 percent compared to 1992."

Kanban, a Japanese term applied to inventory replenishment systems triggered by visual signals, has been a key feature of CLPS efforts in each CTD plant. A kanban system consists of racks that store bins of parts, say washers or bolts, with the quantity of parts in the bins based on historical usage. The bins are staged at the point of use, so when one is empty another comes down to take its place. Line personnel place the empty bins on the top of the rack. The empty bins, marked with a bar-code label and usually colored red, act as a signal to alert material handlers to replenish parts.

According to Mike Embler, manufacturing supervisor, before kanbans were introduced in Athens, line workers had to flag down material handlers when parts were low. The material handlers then filed handwritten parts requests with the warehouse. This time-consuming process often impeded work flow, sometimes causing stoppages of 15-20 minutes on the production line. The kanban system helps overcome that. Material handlers look for the empty-bin signal to see when parts are needed, and while an empty bin is being refilled, another, full one has descended to replace it. When the material handler brings the bin to the warehouse, the warehouse clerk merely scans the bin's bar code to find out everything he or she needs to know: the part number, where the part is in the warehouse, specific quantities required, where the part goes. The Athens facility's main line has 12 individual kanban racks with 900 bins. Ted Cromartie, senior quality engineer, says the plant is now taking this system a step further by having outside suppliers regularly deliver refilled bins directly to the point of use. Having suppliers conform to the kanban system frees up CTD employees to perform other duties.

Besides transforming the way inventory is requisitioned by and supplied to the line, the Athens staff introduced new materials requirement planning procedures. "Before we had MRP, our parts philosophy — like most American factories — was one of 'just don't run out.' Even if you knew that you only needed 10,000 fasteners, you ordered 12,000 just to be safe. So inventory levels were sky high. We never even got close to having a low inventory. Warehousing took up one-third of the plant," says Embler. Today, MRP reports tell line employees how much of a certain part was used, how much is needed next week, supply lead time, etc. And the staff not only views weekly MRP reports, but up-to-the-minute on-line information as well. Now supervisors order not 10,000 at once but 2,000 per week for the next five weeks, thus ensuring supply while minimizing in-house inventory, conserving space and improving cash flow.

Integral to CLPS efforts in restructuring planning and production at Athens was the plant's ISO certification program. Cromartie, who serves as the facility's deputy ISO program manager, says that before the plant was ISO 9000 certified, there were only verbal indications, inconsistent written notices and complicated engineering drawings to inform and remind workers about production processes after the initial training. And not only were the references inadequate and hard to use, old revisions of these materials led to misinformation, which caused rejects, costly rework and missed deadlines. To become ISO 9000 certified, the plant had to establish a controlled process for production, with documented methods for the entire factory. Plant management and engineers developed method sheets to provide user-friendly instruction, with clearly written and diagramed instructions for fabrication and other processes replacing the former blueprint-style illustrations. Revisions are now coded and universal.

"Being ISO 9000 certified means we have a consistent quality framework, a day-in-day-out discipline, with written documentation, training, line calibration and process control," says Cromartie. "There are obvious efficiencies that come from it — especially when flow manufacturing has employees moving between different work stations — but a main reason we pursued it was to attract foreign customers. Foreign customers, especially those in the European Community, look for the discipline and consistency that come from ISO 9000-certified manufacturers."

To Ferguson, the essential aspect of CLPS—beyond instilling new discipline and enhancing production — has been the cultural changes it has wrought, the way it has helped steer employees toward new ways of solving problems. "We've got a lot of employees who have been immersed in the traditional ways of doing things, and we've worked hard to get them to look beyond the horizon. We think we've been 70 percent successful so far, and we're picking up momentum all the time." An example of employees seeking fresh solutions stems from how supplier replenishment has become a chief means of streamlining processes for the plant. The facility's powder paint area now has its vendor supply paint powder in refillable bulk containers instead of delivering it in the 50-pound boxes, which made line workers take time and effort to lift and fit. By getting rid of the heavy, inconvenient boxes, this new method provides benefits not only in terms of improved efficiency and ergonomics but environmentally as well. Supplying four times the paint of a single box, the reusable bulk barrel eliminates 3,200 pounds of waste cardboard per year.

Work-in-progress: cultural change
As with the Athens plant, the other CTD facilities implementing CLPS have each attained significant technical improvements while addressing cultural change issues. At the Syracuse, N.Y., facility, CTD faces challenges because its marine transport refrigeration product is being sold at the same price it was 10 years ago. Ever-increasing efficiency and continual cost-cutting are vital to profitability, though introducing new ways and means has required patience and persuasion.

With the Syracuse plant doubling in number of employees over the past five years, asset management and lowering labor costs have been paramount concerns and the implementation of CLPS their primary amelioration. To lower resistance to the new philosophy and unfamiliar methods, Richard Laubenstein, plant manager, and Dan Behr, CLPS program manager (now production manager for the York, Pa., facility), prescribed 80 hours of training for every employee. The training has served to re-educate the work force technically and acclimate it socially. Courses in cultural orientation, personality profiles, team building and interpersonal skills are accorded the same emphasis as those for flow processes. And to help line workers navigate through the new system, managers and engineers act as "mentors," guiding operating teams in their quest for continuous improvement.

According to Laubenstein, the "here today, gone tomorrow" record of past management programs accompanied by acronyms and hype made enthusiasm for CLPS hard to garner at times. "The employees would say: 'We believe it works; we believe it's a good program. We just don't think you're going to stick with it long enough to make a difference.' It's true. Staying focused is often the biggest challenge. That's where our steering committee comes in. Key managers get together once a week to work at reinforcing enthusiasm and maintaining corporate commitment."

As with the Athens facility, the Syracuse factory began CLPS by converting the assembly line to a flow process with established TAKT times (cycle time based on demand rather than set rates); implementing kanban systems internally and with external suppliers; and instituting method sheets to illustrate work content and quality check points. The reward for the revamping has been substantial, says Laubenstein. Factory lead time decreased; work-in-process inventory turns doubled; delivered product defect rates fell by half; and occupied space decreased by 30 percent while product demand increased by 25 percent.

The same impressive numbers are boasted by the Rouen, France, facility, where via the CLPS program two factories were consolidated into one, 40,000 square feet of inventory storage space was eliminated, and inventory turnover increased by almost 300 percent. According to Colin Martin, manufacturing resource manager, every product line at the plant had its product and manufacturing process reengineered. Instead of separate departments for production, warehousing and subassembly, each product now is produced in a work cell environment. A team concept also accompanies these work cells, replacing traditional supervisor control. These work cells have become such a success that benefits accrue not only to production but marketing as well. Martin says the factory reorganization is a "first-class sales tool. Customers can see the value when they visit; the benefits in quality and timeliness are obvious. They say, 'Why aren't your competitors doing this?'"

The biggest obstacles to these drastic changes and stellar results were again social rather than technical. Says Martin, "Getting employees to forget the old ways is often harder than getting them to learn the new. The cultural issues were tricky. CLPS had to be introduced gradually; the French can be touchy about being told new ways of doing their jobs."

In Mexico City, too, CTD management had to negotiate cultural barriers to realize the advantages of CLPS. According to Mike Latuga, director of manufacturing, the Mexican factory was doing a good job but, with the growth in business they were experiencing, a new approach was needed. The first step on the way to lean production was to organize and change the flow of the plant; next was translating existing instructions for fabrication and assembly into new-and-improved method sheets; then TAKT times were started and kanban systems installed.

The strategy for bridging the cultural gap involved the Mexican employees, literally. The plant staff created a program to foster employee initiative and communication. Instead of translating engineering documentation from English to Spanish, the employees compose their own method sheets for production. Latuga says, "Soon, there were method sheets everywhere. The extra meetings for CLPS yielded the side benefit of improving communication all-around." Incentives in the form of bonuses and prizes were used to motivate team productivity and support of CLPS.

A crucial management technique for promoting cultural change, according to Latuga, was giving the team leader positions to bright young people right off the production floor. "Having the CLPS precepts come from one of the employees' own made the changes more readily received. The new team leader approach helped overcome resistance to change and also helped preserve continuity with the typically high turnover. The team leaders have been so key that we're investing more training in them," says Latuga.

Inventory turns at the Mexico City factory have doubled in the past year. Latuga says near-term goals include increasing productivity by 20-25 percent; reducing warranty claims by 50 percent; and adding new production lines. "Before introducing CLPS, we thought we were going to have to move the plant to meet increased capacity requirements. The initial gains from CLPS enabled us to stay. And, not only that, the gains opened the workers' eyes as to how much more is possible."

Hoping to add to the successes of the Athens, Syracuse, Rouen and Mexico City plants are CTD's AC Industries subsidiary in York, Pa., and TempCon subsidiary in Montreal, where CLPS efforts are under way. The potential profits and pitfalls facing these two subsidiaries are akin to those faced by the other facilities.

The keenest frustration thus far with the CLPS crusade has been the prolonged ramp-up of the plants' empowered work teams.

The consensus seems to be that the new modes of operation weren't accompanied by enough guidance. "We moved a little too fast in some places by setting up empowered work teams without providing enough technical support," Laidman says. "Although they had enough of 'what to do,' they didn't have enough of 'how to do it.' One of our mid-course corrections has been to institute more training as well as more design for manufacturing, such as poke-yoke — the failure-proofing of a process so something can be put together only one way, limiting the number of mistakes that can be made."

Along with similar trials and errors, the subsidiary facilities also can expect to generate benefits beyond the numbers, just as did the first plants to sign on with CLPS. "We've had remarkable savings in assets — inventory, space and better deployment of people — but the most significant advantage of CLPS has been as a rallying point for manufacturing," Laidman says. "With CLPS, there is a clear picture of where we're going. Now we have a common language, common goals."

Investing in the future
To be successful, a BPR program such as CLPS must have explicit support and clear direction from the top. Guy Fauconneau, CTD president, has championed CLPS and the relationship between CTD and UT. A Ph.D. in mechanical engineering and a former professor at the University of Pittsburgh, Fauconneau recognizes the competitive advantages the university provides through its research, training and student internship programs. "It's an innovative way of working that has value for both sides. In the past, people might have used universities only to solve a particular problem. We're not after a neatly wrapped deliverable but rather the overall cultural benefit that comes from the university approach — it pushes us to question and look beyond ourselves. If you stay strictly in the business environment, you can forget that things are evolving on the outside."

CTD/university research projects involve faculty and graduate students working with CTD managers and engineers to develop new concepts to solve old problems, methodologies to carry out the solutions and software to support the implementations. Currently, two major research initiatives are under way. The first program centers on information services, with a CTD/university team devising new business systems and software programs to support scheduling routines, order administration, materials management and distribution. Aiming to integrate new CLPS-oriented processes with CTD's existing MRP procedures, the university develops the theoretical underpinnings, and CTD writes the actual software. Begun in February 1993, the information services program is slated for completion in 1995. The second research initiative revolves around BPR methodology, with the university team striving to lay the theoretical foundation for CTD's reengineering, including activity-based modeling techniques for costs and process flow. Begun in fall 1993, the methodology program should come to fruition in mid-1994.

The training portion of the CTD/university partnership begins with a five-day course in the principles of CLPS for a facility's production leaders. This is followed by a strategic planning workshop with key managers and a series of tactical planning workshops with individual reengineering teams, as well as routinely scheduled progress reviews. Chief subject areas covered in the training include flow manufacturing, rate-based materials management, supplier development and continuous-improvement training.

In addition to research and training, the university supplies CTD with graduate student interns, who work summers with the company to implement CLPS. One such student is Rick Hollander, a UT industrial engineering graduate now in the school's MBA program, who served as an intern at the Syracuse facility. He spent the summer of 1993 helping implement kanban systems at the plant and with certain of its suppliers. Now he is working to develop the concept statement for the CTD/university information systems project.

Interns like Hollander symbolize the value of a university relationship over an arrangement with a traditional consulting firm, according to Greenwood. "The benefits of a university relationship are much broader than those of a typical consulting firm when you consider the university-based research with its access to a wide range of information and leading-edge technologies," he says. "And with interns, companies get exposure to young people who are qualified and very focused at cost-effective rates. By using graduate interns, you're hopefully grooming someone with the potential to come into the company — someone who is not only well educated but who already has experience with the company... It's investing in the future."

Not only are today's interns possibly tomorrow's managers and engineers, they are enthusiastic contributors and immediate assets as well, says Hollander. "As an intern, I was looking for answers as well as trying to give them. So that made me, I think, more aware of all sides of a problem — I was able to get deeper into it. Also, I had nothing to lose by trying new things, as opposed to a consultant who might operate a bit safer."

Along with value and enthusiasm, according to Laidman, the CTD/university alliance reflects a versatility often lacking in the standard corporate approach to outside assistance. "Many times, a consultant comes in with a standard package, and you end up revising your processes to fit the package: sort of, 'If you do it my way, it'll work and there'll be no problems.' University people tend to have a more open attitude to making solutions fit the company, instead of the other way around.

"Also, a consulting firm usually has a good history of 'wins,' but its experience may be more narrowly focused — they're specialists in something," Laidman continues. "A university generally has more adaptable expertise. Sometimes the consultant's package is the smart thing to do — we have used and do use consultants, too, at times — but when we're treading new waters like we are with CLPS, I think the more broad-minded, flexible approach is the way to go."

From the results CTD has gained through researching, training and implementing CLPS with UT, it seems that the school indeed has been an institution of higher learning for the company. The numbers speak for themselves, says Greenwood. "Michael Hammer's examples in his book [*Reengineering the Corporation*] don't hold a candle to the gains we've made, like 200 to 300 percent improvement in inventory turns, 50 to 100 percent improvements in key quality indices and quantum increases in just about every measure of productivity. What this translates into is that CTD's customers are better served through CLPS, and the plants are better places to work."

A
Case Study
by
Brad Bambarger

Corning Asahi Video Products Co.

What had been a state-of-the-art order-processing system in the mid-1970s for Corning Asahi Video Products Co. (CAV) had become a dinosaur by the early 1990s, a monster responsible for massive errors in order fulfillment. Delivery trucks arrived with the wrong product or, on occasion, not at all, stressing customer production cycles to the breaking point. Missed billings and inaccurate discounts also bled thousands of dollars from CAV's receivables. These mistakes in distribution, delivery and billing were eating up $2 million per year — a conservative estimate — in overtime hours, additional freight charges, extra phone calls and faxes, production rework and give-aways, not to mention the awful expense of defecting customers. And with the antiquated software, processes and attitudes in place, this nightmare scenario stood to only get worse.

It took an intensive business process reengineering (BPR) program to reinvent CAV's order fulfillment system and restore customer satisfaction. And what a BPR program it was. From summer 1991 to early 1993, the CAV reengineering team achieved a zero defect ratio, thereby surpassing its goal of reducing the cost of errors by $1.6 million — it eliminated the entire $2 million cost. The team also met its goal of reducing head count by restructuring the department and eliminating four full-time positions for a savings of $400,000 per year.

One of those displaced employees was reengineering team leader Maggie Coffey, who worked her way out of a job as CAV's customer service manager. Now an internal reengineering consultant with parent company Corning Inc.'s corporate systems engineering group, Coffey says, "Sometimes major change leaves a bad taste in people's mouths, but with this project people felt very good about the outcome. I think [BPR guru Michael] Hammer is right when he says that the true litmus test for a successful reengineering program isn't in head count or the money saved. It's when someone who gets displaced by it says, 'I totally understand the business imperative at work here. I know my job being cut was in the best interest, and I would definitely come back to work here if there were an open spot.' "

In addition to Maggie being offered a new position, one of the other employees whose jobs vanished because of the reengineering received an attractive early retirement offer, and the other two were redeployed to other Corning divisions. Testimonials for the program's positive effects have come from not only satisfied customers but from CAV employees, who, Coffey says, are more satisfied with their jobs because they are now able to satisfy the customers.

The BPR project's success generated a ripple effect of enthusiasm that flowed from the order fulfillment department across the whole company, indicated by the reengineering team being honored with the 1993 Corning Quality award for the most outstanding contribution to quality within the company, presented by the president of Corning and voted on by employees from a field of more than 100 nominees. In addition, Corning has announced a corporate-wide reengineering program. That sort of management reinforcement along with the employee-mandated award may seem like the ultimate validation for a team's efforts, but, for Coffey, that came from a smaller, more personal encounter.

"I think the best postmortem I've gotten on the project was from a CAV employee who is thought of as the company pessimist," says Coffey. "He said, 'That reengineering team is the most excellent group of people I've ever worked with. They really came through; our customers are so pleased.' That statement coming from someone for whom the glass is always 'half empty' made me very proud."

Reengineering fulfillment

One of Corning's oldest and largest business units, CAV is a State College, Pa.-based, 1,200-employee firm that manufactures television tubes. Prior to the BPR project, order processing was entered at CAV corporate, with a computer print-out then sent to the manufacturing facility. From then on, it was a manual process, with factory personnel physically checking, picking and tagging inventory with no comput-

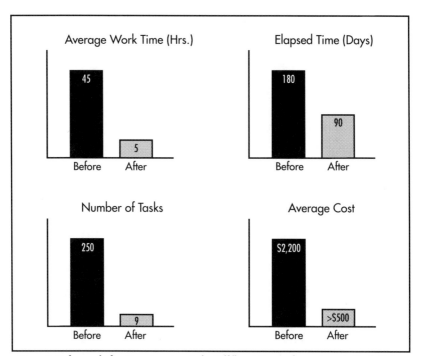

Figure 1. Before and After Reengineering; Order-Fulfillment Process for an Average Single Order

erized data on which to rely. Hand work took much time, and the rekeying of information at different points incurred many errors. There also was no cross training or data backup. If someone left or was sick, information and service for that person's account was locked up in his or her personal filing system (see figure 1).

At one time, 20 to 25 people had a hand in the logistics of the process. With the reinvention of the order fulfillment process, four people now "own" the new process. And, according to Coffey, customer service reps are no longer considered clerical workers but entry-level management. Reengineering also reduced the average work time necessary to fulfill an order from 45 hours per order to only five. The number of days required to process an order was slashed by half, from 180 days to 90. The number of tasks needed to fulfill an order was cut from 250 to nine. The cost per order went from $2,200 to less than $500. And the price for all these results came to $985,000 — $400,000 for internal personnel hours, $418,000 for external personnel hours and $167,000 for hardware and software.

In the project's formative phase, Coffey, a Harvard MBA grad, invited Harvard Business School organizational change specialist Michael Beer — formerly a member of Corning's human resource

department when it first began to set up self-managed work teams —
to visit CAV and deliver a lecture to the redesign team on the
opportunities and obstacles inherent in BPR, a session Coffey describes as a day of "shock therapy." Soon after, Coffey met with
Michael Hammer and CSC/Index, whose theories about how to
pursue change in business matched those of Coffey and her colleagues. And though CAV did not hire Hammer as a consultant, his
blessing of the team's plan helped galvanize the project.

The redesign team was cross-functional, consisting of 13
members from customer service, sales, information services, engineering, logistics planning and manufacturing sites. (The team
added members for the project's implementation phase.) The team
redesigned the order fulfillment process during an intense 15 days
off-site — an atypical move in the days before reengineering was a
corporate buzz word, Coffey says. "Now it seems pretty traditional
what we did, meeting away from the office full-time for more than two
weeks, but back then it was pretty unusual." See figure 2 for timeline.

In redesigning the process, Coffey's team relied on three
established Corning project management methodologies — Innovation, IMPACT and Solution — adapting these to fresh reengineering
concepts. "Because they were readily understood, accepted Corning
tools, it made the reengineering easier to get across to management
and other departments."

Attempting to minimize investment risk, Innovation looks at
the introduction of a new product or process, breaking it down to five
steps: gaining knowledge, determining feasibility, testing practicality
and proving profitability. At the end of each of the steps, the process
helps you determine "go" or "no go" according to a defined cost-
benefit ratio.

Corning's IMPACT (Improvement Method for Process Analysis of Cost-Time) consists of developing commitment to a project,
selecting teams, analyzing the current process, targeting improvements, redesigning the process and implementing the new system.
Before the order fulfillment BPR project, the IMPACT methodology
was used mainly at the work station level to improve existing processes.
Coffey's team expanded the tool's scope to encompass a cross-
functional, "green field" scenario, not only eliminating nonvalue-
added steps but completely reinventing processes.

Solution, a problem-solving tool adapted from a model
created by the Princeton, N.J.-based organizational development
consultancy Kepner-Tregoe Inc., helps users understand the issues

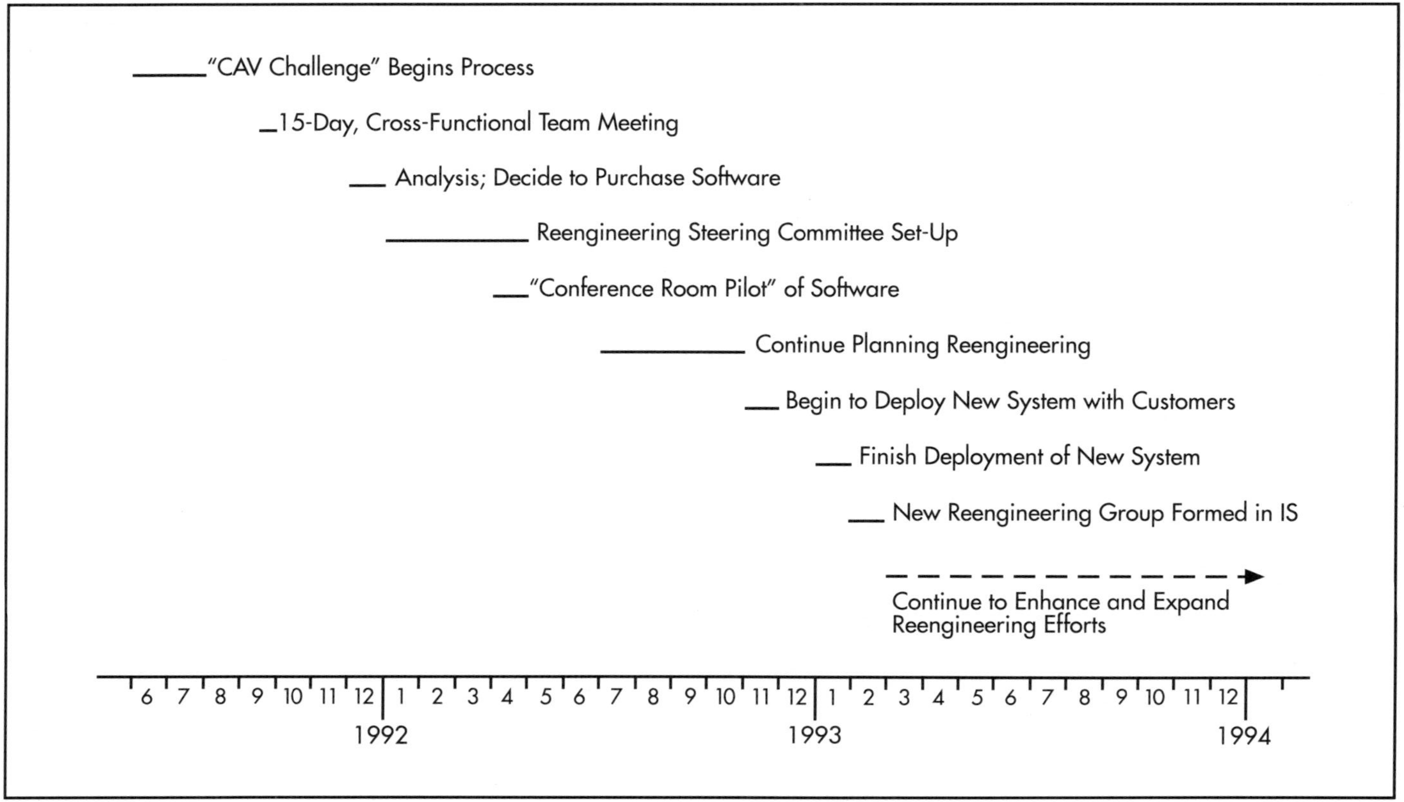

Figure 2. Timeline

behind a problem, examine cause and effect, and prioritize action. After redesigning the department's processes with these methodologies, the team made sure the new processes complied with both Baldrige TQM criteria and ISO 9000 standards. In fact, Coffey says, "When the ISO reviewers came, they said that our department was the first in the company to measure up to ISO 9000 by having our processes thoroughly documented."

Software solutions
After thoroughly analyzing the existing process and redesigning it according to key goals, Coffey's team decided to go with an outside software solution rather than relying on the usual Corning-developed, customized software. Coffey says the project's deadline pressures and cost constraints did not allow for the company to develop software from within. But going with an outside, off-the-shelf software package was counter to the Corning culture and required careful consideration.

After much deliberation, the vendor of choice was narrowed to the Chicago-based consulting firm Arthur Andersen and its DCS Logistics package. According to Walt Surdak, CAV information services director, one of the main reasons for considering DCS Logistics was that it worked with CAV's existing hardware, a VAX mainframe-type platform by Digital Equipment Corp. Also, performance-wise, the system allowed for access to real-time inventory data and linkages with Corning's financial system; with the new system, orders had to be received, processed and shipped with a one-time, universal entry of information.

Even with the benefits of the software package, final decisions were difficult. "It was new, complex — there was some risk involved. Even though, with the extent of our system, it was going to be painful no matter which software we chose. But because the software was so new, and there was so little experience in the market place with this sort of [VAX] application, that made it worse. Although [Arthur Andersen] obviously did a good job of testing and debugging the package, we still didn't know what to expect — we would be the pioneers who got the arrows" says Surdak.

Visiting another company that used the Andersen software on a VAX system helped allay some fears, enabling the team to see how actual problems were resolved to yield benefits from the technology. "Going there, we learned that the company's sales reps initially felt threatened by all the info that was now in the hands of its customer service reps," Surdak recalls. "When you empower one group the perception often is that you're taking power away from another group. There's also a natural tension that comes with this in that people are thinking, 'This may be good for the customer, but is it bad for us?' But in this case, the system actually made the sales reps jobs easier by eliminating administrative drudgery and reducing customer complaints."

The key determinant for going with DCS Logistics stemmed from Andersen consultants coming in to perform a "conference room pilot." They loaded CAV's data into the system and helped the order fulfillment department run a seven-week on-site test to determine if the software would meet CAV's needs. The trial's success impressed the project steering committee, which gave the go-ahead for the BPR team to purchase DCS Logistics and begin implementing the new system. With this, employees began to receive three months of training on the new system and started working to write the operation manual.

Surdak explains that information services benefits reengineering projects like this because IS typically knows the functional area as well as the technology that helps the function work. "Technology plays a pervasive role in all business processes today; so, typically, computer systems play a part in nearly every reengineering solution," he says. "But having said that, I don't think technology is the answer. Computers aren't a magic bullet but a facilitator. Computers can't replace human beings; they can only help make them more effective. We can't forget that."

In the past, there has been an assumption among some internal IS customers, Surdak says, that the department "has the answers before we know the questions, but that is exactly what we try not to do. We come with technological know-how, a knowledge of how the function operates and its needs, as well as a knowledge of the many alternatives available out there — which we gather by benchmarking other companies' reengineering solutions. We try to integrate the needs of our internal customers with the technology available."

Surdak says that it is projects such as this that show how reengineering has become a primary focus for IS. "We've taken a leadership role at Corning and been relatively successful. We're gaining credibility, but we're still closer to the beginning than we are to the end. We've got a ways to go... But now people are more comfortable with major change and that allows us to help them easier and more effectively.

"We've gone from untouchable or out-of-touch experts in a 'glass house' — in a room by ourselves with a mainframe — to being partners with other departments to solve problems," he adds. "And BPR provides the vehicle for building the trust between IS and the other departments that makes that possible."

Hindsight observations

Even when a BPR project generates impressive numbers and positive feelings like this one, it is often when speaking of obstacles hurdled that insights for future reengineering ensue. Ruth Riesbeck, then quality coordinator for CAV, now manager of quality and administration for Corning Engineering, says among the project's primary challenges was convincing employees to step outside their previous frames of reference. "Getting people to think out-of-the-box, not being burdened by personal or functional biases, to bust out of their paradigms and come up with the ideal methodology — we had a tough time with that," she says. "You have to think about what could be not what can be."

Riesbeck also points out that a lack of time was a particular hindrance in this project. "We initially established the team to represent the organization, which is smart for a redesign team," Riesbeck explains. "But what we discovered was that in figuring out what exactly the process was then — understanding complaints and problems — we found out that we didn't have any common processes across the organization. So to truly understand the process, we had to talk to everyone. We had to have a tag team approach of getting all the customer service people rotating off their workstations to tell their stories. In the ideal reengineering situation, you should be able to pull people out of their jobs completely to concentrate on the problem 8 to 5 every day until the problem is solved. But our problem was so pervasive that we didn't have anyone to backfill on the line for those who were working on the reengineering.

"What I would like to have next time would be a block of time set aside for intensive training prior to the initial redesign meetings," Riesbeck adds. "Training on just what reengineering is, how to get from point A to point B. And for people to break out of their paradigms, that takes time and training. Plus, team members have to be trained on how to work together as a team, suppressing egos and cooperating more… In the end, we got to that point, but if we had done the training beforehand, it would definitely have been easier and maybe faster."

Coffey concurs that addressing reluctance to change and resistance to new methods takes the time and trouble of talking, and plenty of it. "We worked for a long time — more than a year — in the redesign, software selection, organizational change, implementation and start-up, and we faced a lot of skepticism, a lot of resistance," she says. "Back then, BPR wasn't in the media like it is now. We got resistance from both middle management and the rank and file. But you know what they say are the most important aspects of any BPR program — communication, communication and communication. That's true. Explaining things clearly and involving people and valuing their input are the keys to breaking down resistance."

One thing that helped assuage the project's pressures was support from the top, Riesbeck says. "Ken Freeman [then president of CAV, now an executive vice president with Corning Inc.] came in from time to time and talked to us about the reengineering. He just came in and said, 'What's happening?' and 'I support what you're doing.' Those pep talks were invaluable."

The success of CAV's BPR initiative success has helped change become more readily accepted in Corning, from the bottom to the top, says Coffey. "It's been a major cultural achievement. Our program was a catalyst for the new major Corning corporate reengineering initiative now under way. BPR and major change are business as usual now."

But with the benefit of hindsight, Coffey sees definite room for improvement. "Sometimes, I feel bad when I read about other companies' reengineering teams and how they celebrate their projects with t-shirts, banners and victory parties. We never celebrated. We worked hard, finished up and moved on. I feel like we should whoop it up a bit more about our successes."

A
Case Study
by
Susan Taylor

Eastman Chemical Company

At Eastman Chemical Company, being world class just is not good enough. The company has set its sights on being the preferred chemical company in the world, a goal that requires a level of operating performance in a class by itself.

When an internal survey revealed that maintenance staff were spending as much as 50 percent of their time finding and ordering equipment parts, Eastman knew the time had come for radical change. After a massive reengineering effort that took nearly three years, Eastman has cut by 80 percent the time needed to find and order materials. As a result, maintenance productivity has risen sharply, equipment uptime has increased and the company is saving more than $1 million every year in duplicate inventory costs.

Since that first project was completed, Eastman has embraced business process reengineering (BPR) as a key strategy to give the company a significant competitive edge. The company has in place a top level BPR strategy team and an active internal training program. Specific BPR projects underway now are aimed at those areas, such as pricing policies, customer interfaces, order management systems and product development cycles, that Eastman believes will make it the world's preferred chemical company.

Quantum leap in quality processes

Headquartered in Kingsport, Tenn., Eastman manufactures and markets more than 400 different chemicals, fibers and plastics in 80 countries. 1992 sales were almost $4 billion, ranking the company as the 10th largest chemical producer in the U.S. Besides Kingsport,

Eastman also has manufacturing plants at Batesville, Ark.; Columbia, S.C.; and Longview, Texas.

Eastman's status as a unit of Eastman Kodak Co. ended when Kodak completed a spin-off that made Eastman Chemical Company a separate corporate entity for the first time. This new corporate identity brings its own set of opportunities and challenges, and Eastman management already is planning a long-term strategy that recognizes the importance of customer focus, market leadership, individual unit profits and accountability to shareholders. BPR is an integral part of that strategy.

Long before the spin-off was conceived, however, Eastman management was conscious of the need to maintain market leadership by constantly re-examining operations and processes that impact customer satisfaction. In the early 1980s, the company began a process-focused Total Quality Management (TQM) program, which continues today. The goal of this program is for each organization within Eastman to recognize how it adds value to the overall business process that makes a difference to the external customer. Figure 1 illustrates the importance of customer focus in Eastman's quality management process

As part of the TQM program, industrial engineers from the internal management engineering services group work as quality consultants to the various organizations within Eastman to help them develop a value-added perspective. In 1985, the stores and supplies organization formed a business strategy group and began developing a three-year vision and plan of how it would add value to Eastman and, "If you look at maintenance effectiveness, it was ridiculous," says Bob Savell, the senior management engineer who worked as a quality consultant with stores. "We're talking about hundreds of mechanics spending this much of their time before they can even begin repairing the equipment. Once they had the materials and parts they needed, they got the job done really well."

The survey also showed that maintenance staff in different locations had different approaches to getting materials. Some would go "shopping" in the local maintenance storeroom, taking items off the shelf and often putting them back in the wrong place. Others would call on the phone. Some used card systems with catalogs and parts lists, but these systems often did not reflect latest corrections and updates. Some maintenance shops even kept their own local inventories. The most modern system at the time was based on microfiche catalogs; however, this system was slow, difficult to use and not maintained effectively area-by-area.

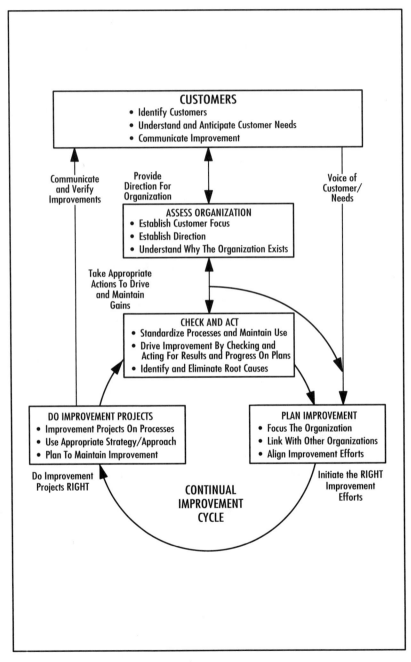

Figure 1. Quality Management Process

"The survey got us to recognize we had a big problem and a big opportunity," Savell says. "We knew we would have to start from scratch to redesign the process. We couldn't improve what we had by tweaking this hodgepodge of systems. We had to totally take it away and start over. We didn't call it business process reengineering because we didn't know that term at the time. But that's what it was.

"There are two things you have to have to do effective BPR. You must have a vision of where you are going, and you need a case for action," he continues. "As a result of this study, we developed a vision of where we wanted to go and why, and also what that meant from a business perspective.

"This project was primarily driven because of complexities, costs and trying to streamline the way we do things internally so that we can, in fact, serve our customers better. If you think of the amount of time mechanics were tied up in an information-based process just to get the parts they needed, you realize that was keeping them from repairing equipment, keeping equipment from running and keeping the plant from being reliable, which directly relates to our ability to service our customers. And if we can make the plant more reliable, we don't need as many stores inventories to back up that reliability. So the cost ramifications were huge."

Using a procedure that echoes Michael Hammer's "clean sheet" approach, the stores strategy group started from scratch to come up with the ideal stores/customer interface. The group concluded that the ideal would be for a mechanic, regardless of where he was in the facility, to go to a nearby terminal, enter a number from the equipment tag, and be able to see on the screen a parts list and maybe graphics or whatever he needed to identify the parts necessary to repair that piece of equipment. The mechanic also could see where those parts were stored at Eastman and could order them so they would be delivered when and where he needed them.

"The goal was to take a quantum leap forward to improve a very large and costly internal customer interface," Savell explains. "We wanted to radically change this internal customer interface. Once we made the shift, we wanted to standardize on that improvement so we wouldn't fall back, and then manage the process for continual improvement and change."

Champions throughout the organization

The stores group knew that accomplishing the vision would take cooperation from functions throughout the organization, including but not limited to stores, maintenance, information systems, engineering and purchasing. The next step then, was to enlist commitment from top management to cut across those functional boundaries and provide a total business perspective.

Since stores reported to Jim Hall, who was division head of shops and services, he was given the vision and enlisted as the management-level project champion. As champion, Hall worked to get the vice president level staff to buy into the project and provide their support.

Hall also put together and led a cross-functional team to help make the change take place. The team included the director of maintenance, plus division level managers from engineering, information systems, and the department head from electrical and instruments.

"We had some heated discussions," says Roger Tittle, director of information systems at the time, "but most people took off their functional hats and were more looking at the whole process, rather than ownership issues. That was really critical to our success."

Hall also recognized that the whole maintenance organization would have to buy into the project as an equal partner. He had the stores group make a "sales pitch" to maintenance, sharing with them what had been found in the surveys and what the potential benefits were for them.

"We had to make a change occur for a very large number of people, and we had to orchestrate it in such a way that they felt they were part of the change — not driven, but doing the driving," Savell says. "That's probably the most important aspect of change management. People are willing to change if they feel they have control."

The maintenance department head was asked to help select a second project champion, this time from within the maintenance ranks. This champion needed to be a first or second level supervisor who had come up through the ranks and who was well thought of by his peers and also by the mechanics. This person would carry the banner for maintenance, while serving as an internal change agent within maintenance because people believed him.

Joe Watson met all the criteria and was enlisted in this role. He had worked extensively with the existing system and understood the problems. Watson also believed strongly in good equipment spare parts catalogs and had one of the best individual systems at Eastman at that time. In addition, he had the kind of integrity that made people listen to him.

Cross-functional teams redesign process

With a change champion in place at both levels, Eastman put together another cross-functional team to redesign the process. This seven-member team included representatives from stores, maintenance, information systems, instruments, and the plants at Columbia and Batesville, as well as the consultant from management engineering services (MES). (The Longview plant was not included in the original design because of computer system incompatibility at the time.) These representatives were chosen for their expertise and ability in their respective areas.

"One thing that made the project go as well as it did was that the system design actually was done by the users," explains Tittle. "It was more of a partnership arrangement than a system driven by the information systems group — which up until then was how most projects were done."

Tittle emphasizes, however, that the systems group must be involved early in a BPR project because information technology is such a big part of the success. "You can come up with ideas to change the work process, but if you don't have the system to do it — well, that's the tool that allows you to do the work," he adds.

A key stakeholder advisory team also was formed to provide user input to the core design team on key design elements. This larger advisory team was made up of stores and maintenance representatives from all the areas involved, including the acid division, cellulose esters division and polymers division at Kingsport, and the two other plant sites. Because the new system had to allow for adding and managing spare parts for new equipment, representatives from engineering and purchasing also were included on the advisory team.

"From a change perspective, we engaged people from all geographic areas," Savell explains. "This was not something that was going to be done to Arkansas by Tennessee. Each area was made a full partner, with the same number of votes. Again, that made them feel like they were driving, rather than being driven. It was another key element in our success."

Eastman also recognized that long-term success meant managing the new system as part of an ongoing quality process. After implementation, members of the design team would become the materials information group (MIG), a six-person process management team responsible for maintaining the integrity of the data and the consistency of the indices.

"The accuracy and usage of the system is totally dependent on the accuracy of the information in the database, and how it is maintained by a central group of people," says Savell. "We knew that we could spend man-years worth of effort to get all our indices right, get all spare parts data correct, all equipment data correct, and get it in the computer system; but if we didn't have a means of managing and maintaining it, it would be just a matter of months before it would be useless again."

"One of the hardest things we had to sell to management was the fact that they had to be willing to put this many people, full time forever, to manage a process that didn't belong to any individual one of them," he adds. "It didn't belong to maintenance, stores, engineering or purchasing. It was a company process.

"The only way to sell that was to show them the amount of time mechanics were spending to try to do this. The potential was millions of dollars a year in savings in the way we do business."

Productivity up, costs down

Even with top management support and critical user acceptance, Eastman knew the task would be far from easy. Many obstacles were identified during the design phase of the Equipment Spare Parts Index System (ESPIS). Among other things, the design team had to:

- define the proper organization ownership of the spare parts and materials catalogs;
- develop standard equipment identifications to be used by maintenance, engineering and operations;
- integrate three different computer systems and create a user-friendly computer environment;
- standardize diverse methods of identifying and locating spare parts;
- establish usable, easy-to-understand indices to materials information; and
- coordinate with all remote locations.

The ESPIS project had a critical advantage in that maintenance already was in the process of implementing computerized maintenance information systems for all Eastman operations. New terminals were being put in maintenance shops, and mechanics were being trained to use them as an everyday part of their jobs. The new stores project could be readily piggybacked on that project, thus leveraging a major technology cost in terms of equipment and training.

The design team got started in 1985, and 2.5 years later, the vision was a reality. "We have had a greater than 80 percent reduction in cycle time from the point when a mechanic receives a work order to identifying the materials he needs to get the work done," Savell says.

"Compared with the old hodgepodge of systems, the amount of time spent finding and ordering parts is almost nil," adds Jack Stacy, a member of the MIG. "Before, a mechanic often spent 30 to 40 minutes getting ready to place a materials order. Now, it takes just a couple of minutes to have all the information in hand and actually place the order."

As a result, maintenance productivity at Eastman has increased dramatically, allowing the company to greatly expand its facilities without adding maintenance staff.

In many ways, the project has been more successful than anyone dared hope at the beginning. User acceptance has been growing steadily from the very beginning and measurable cost savings have been significant.

ESPIS was created originally for spare parts, and the designers thought a natural extension would be all mechanical materials, such as janitorial supplies. However, the system works so well for finding generic materials, it has been expanded to all general stores. Everyone at Eastman, whether it is a secretary ordering paper and pencils or a mechanic ordering a very specific control valve, uses the same system to get materials.

"We planned for around 1,800 users originally, but that has grown to between 4,000 and 4,500," comments Richard Harris, another MIG member. "That's a significant percentage of Eastman's total of around 17,000 employees." The system also has been expanded to include about 200,000 individual item numbers.

System acceptance is highest at the South Carolina plant, with 94 percent of all stores requests coming in via ESPIS. Usage at Arkansas is at 75 percent and growing. At Kingsport, utilization is in the high 90s for maintenance and 86 percent for all users. Under the old hodgepodge approach, it took five telephone operators just to answer the phones in stores at Kingsport. Today, thanks to ESPIS, the few phone requests are answered by a machine, and those former phone operators can be more effective at controlling inventory accuracy and improving the overall stores operation.

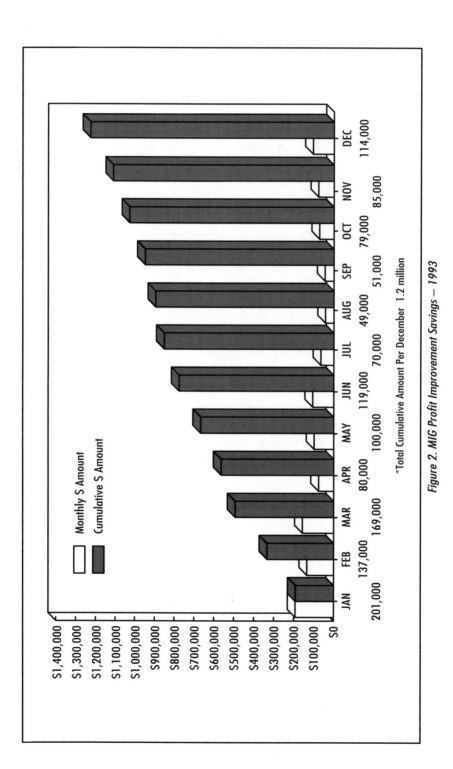

*Total Cumulative Amount Per December 1.2 million

Figure 2. MIG Profit Improvement Savings — 1993

Harris also points out that, with the MIG managing the process in a quality fashion, Eastman is saving more than $1 million a year in duplicate materials requests. Figure 2 shows that cumulative savings for the first seven months of 1993 add up to almost $900,000.

Eastman now is in the process of implementing SAP software running in IMS DB2 to handle all its systems world-wide. Since ESPIS is written in IMS DB2, it can be interfaced easily with the new system. Once SAP is fully implemented, the Longview plant will begin using ESPIS as well.

BPR as a way of life

Although the ESPIS project was not called BPR at the time, Eastman has incorporated many of the key elements from this first project into its current BPR program. This includes the need to enlist change champions at the top and bottom levels, use cross-functional teams both in management and in design, and manage each specific project as an ongoing quality process.

BPR as a corporate-wide strategy began in earnest three years ago at Eastman when the company went through a business strategy journey to define its corporate vision and develop a plan to achieve it. Out of that journey came the vision statement, "We want to be the preferred chemical company in the world." A sense of needing to be better than world class pervades the company. That, in turn, is driving the case for action for BPR. While the ESPIS project came out of a vision for change from one functional area, Eastman's current BPR program is driven by an overall business strategy vision.

Eastman also is in the unique position of being able to re-create itself as a spin-off from Kodak. "This environment is very conducive to rewriting the book," says Savell. "Top executives at Eastman are saying we *should* do things differently. There is a sense of urgency to be a different company. It's the best of both worlds: we are on our own, but we still have the Kodak reputation behind us to a degree."

Several other factors have been part of the driving force behind a corporate BPR program at Eastman. These factors include an ongoing emphasis on quality, key management support, pursuit of a Malcolm Baldrige Award, the industrial engineering technology base within the company and an increasingly competitive global marketplace.

Founded in quality — Eastman's BPR program has its roots in the ten-year-old TQM program and the accompanying drive to stay customer process focused. In fact, Eastman calls its program Breakthrough Quality Management/Business Process Reengineering, or BQM/BPR.

"We never limited our quality management efforts to just incremental change," Savell explains. "We encouraged breakthrough efforts. We encouraged the concept of getting a new piece of paper and starting from scratch back in 1981 and '82 when we started our quality program. I will challenge people vehemently who say BPR is totally different and totally separate from quality efforts. You will kill it [BPR], and kill it fast, if you have a quality-oriented company and don't integrate [quality and BPR] and show how they fit together and work together," he adds.

Key management support — Key management recognized the need for change to achieve the new vision, but they knew the change process would have to be managed well to be successful. BPR also would have to be pursued in a way that would fit Eastman's culture. Unlike some companies, Eastman does not have a single BPR "czar," but instead has a team leading the process.

"We are a team-oriented company," says Savell. "There are top management leaders, but with shared responsibility."

The executive BPR team includes representatives from all administrative areas within the company, including human resources, finance, information systems, worldwide sales, supplies and distribution, product support services and legal. The quality coordinator also is on the team because of the need to maintain a quality focus at all times. This executive team determines which specific BPR projects will be undertaken, and acts as the top level change agent. The team works around turf battles by helping to avoid a unit focus and concentrating on "wearing a company hat."

Three team members, in particular, have been very instrumental in recognizing the need and building a case for action for BPR at Eastman. Fielding Rolston, vice president of supplies and distribution, originally recognized the need for a more cross-functional, Eastman-wide perspective on quality projects. He initiated efforts to develop cross-functional teams that would address large business processes.

Jack Spurgeon, chief information officer, also drove BPR from the outset. Spurgeon's staff began attending Michael Hammer forums back in the 1980s when they first started. He also recognized that, as CIO, he could not make BPR happen. Instead, he has concentrated on educating top management through internal and off-site programs. He also brings an invaluable information technology perspective and has been at the forefront in developing strategic information technology architecture that supports BPR.

The third key individual driving BPR is Billy Dickson, who leads a newly created business organization called Product Support Services. As part of its new business strategy, Eastman has reorganized from a product-stream focus to a customer and market focus. The new organization includes 12 business organizations comprising two groups: the Industrial Business Group and the Specialty Business Group. Dickson sits between these two groups and coordinates those things that go across many lines. This puts him in a unique position to see those large cross-functional business processes, as well as those things that impact customers.

Malcolm Baldrige Award — In mid-August 1993, Eastman had a site visit from the Malcolm Baldrige examiners. "Our pursuit of the national quality award pinpointed that Eastman needed to address business processes and gain results in those processes from a quality emphasis," Savell says. "Pursuing that award helped us build a case for action to do some of these projects. We feel we are already winners whether we win the award or not, because of our quality efforts and the results we've seen."

(Editor's note: In October 1993, it was announced that Eastman Chemical Company was one of only two recipients of the 1993 Malcolm Baldrige National Quality Award.)

Industrial engineering base — The industrial engineering technology base within Eastman also has been a driving force behind BPR. Rather than use outside consultants, Eastman chose to train its internal management engineering services group to serve as internal consultants on BPR projects. The company believes its culture is best supported by these internal consultants who understand both the people and the processes involved. The cost for on-going support from outside consultants also would have been prohibitive, the company believes.

Explaining the IE role at Eastman, Savell says, "We are change agent consultants within the organization. We have been developing and working with this type of technology for the past seven or eight years. We help from the educational standpoint — the process improvement standpoint — rather than the information technology standpoint."

Eastman has developed a 3.5-day course for training these internal consultants. The course strives to teach consultants to under-

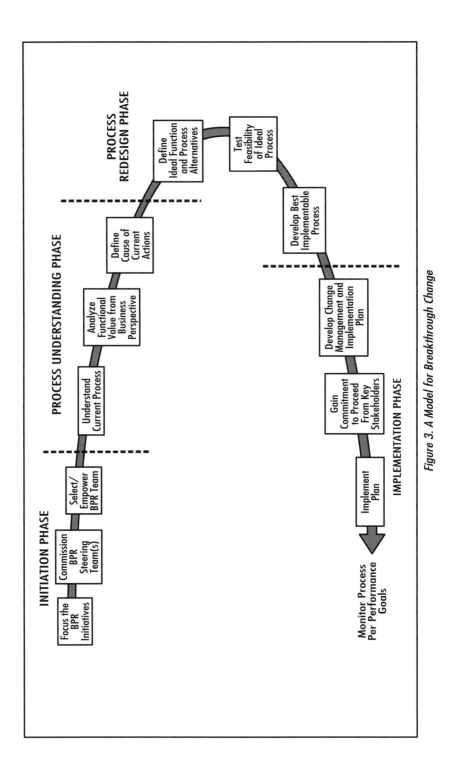

Figure 3. A Model for Breakthrough Change

stand and be able to communicate the concept of BPR and the critical role of information technology, as well as how BPR supports Eastman's major improvement initiatives. The consultants also are taught to apply Eastman's four-phase BPR methodology, as outlined in figure 3. As a result of the training, consultants are able to:

- work with management to initiate a BPR project;
- apply function and value analyses to understand the process being redesigned;
- radically redesign the process using the "ideals" concept and process mapping; and
- lead a team in developing an effective change management plan that includes process documentation, job descriptions, organization proposal, management systems and an information technology plan.

So far, 16 IEs have completed the course, and the company hopes eventually to train everyone in the MES group to assist in BPR.

Global competition — A final element driving the BPR case for action at Eastman has been the changing nature of global business and competition. "Like other companies, we recognize that competition is changing. Quality is almost a given; if you don't have a quality product, you're not even in the game," Savell says. "But competition is heating up and becoming increasingly global.

"In the past, we had some real advantages with some of our processes, but the industry has caught up," he continues. "Now we have to make the next quantum leap. We have to challenge ourselves to jump out and move forward. We're going to do this with BPR."

Organized for change

To make that next competitive quantum leap, Eastman's executive BPR team has pinpointed those processes with the greatest potential for impact and which drive forcefully toward the corporate vision. The major focus is on those processes that touch customers and make it easy for them to do business with Eastman. Initial projects will impact pricing policies, customer interfaces, product development cycles and order management systems, among others.

The company has organized and developed a four-phase BPR model to achieve breakthrough change. The first two phases, initiation and process understanding, focus primarily on problem analysis. As figure 3 shows, the turnaround toward success begins in the process redesign phase, and breakthrough change is fully realized in the final implementation phase.

For each specific project, the executive team names a management steering team. This steering team is responsible for identifying and commissioning a design team, along with a team leader, to re-do the process.

"You have to have great teams to be successful," Savell explains. "You need people willing to exploit change, who have enthusiasm and who may prove to be a little wild.

"Right now, we are constrained by our ability to form teams with the right people," he added. "The problem is getting the right people from the key functions to work on the redesign for at least 50 percent of their time over a significant period of time. Management has accepted that problem and will set priorities and reallocate people as they believe things are most important."

Eastman has found that full-time teams work best. Design teams working part time, while keeping up with their regular job functions, tend to lose focus because of work distractions. Under these circumstances, the design process inevitably takes longer and is much harder to do.

The company also has found that it takes four to eight weeks to assemble a good design team. The management steward over the area to be re-designed is the expert on who would be best on the team. The team leader is especially critical. This individual must be a change agent who also understands the cost of failure.

"A problem with BPR can be expecting too much too soon without a horrendous effort to get it done," Savell says. "You need a focus and a level of determination that is unsurpassed or you will get discouraged. You need a team leader who is very tenacious, who says 'there is no such thing as failure.'"

Two BPR consultants from MES are assigned to each design team. These consultants are chosen for their familiarity with the area to be re-designed and also for their relative age and experience.

"We include one consultant who knows the company, knows the people and knows how to get things done in the existing organization," says Savell. The ideal second consultant is a challenger who is eager to learn and ready to think "out of the box."

An IT person also is included on all teams to provide insight into available technology and how it would work best with Eastman's existing systems.

The design team is then charged with the responsibility to

start with a clean sheet of paper and come up with the ideal process. They must define both the technical and social requirements to reach that ideal, and then develop a plan of change to make that happen. "Then we simply work the plan," says Savell.

In addition to the change model outlined in figure 3, Eastman uses an empowerment model as a checking process. This model reminds the company to ask continually, "Do we have an empowered work force? Do they know and understand their purpose? Do they have the right skills and knowledge to do their jobs (capability)? Do they have a vehicle to remove obstacles and barriers (opportunity)? Do they have the desire and the commitment to get the job done?" These four elements carry equal weight and must operate within an environment conducive to getting the work done.

Focused in the right direction
Although the ESPIS project can be counted as a major success, Eastman is still at the very beginning of its official BPR program. With details related to the spin-off still to be worked out, the company must concentrate on many other areas of business strategy. However, the dedication to BPR is still there.

"At Eastman, management has asked us to be obnoxious, like external consultants would be, to keep them focused and in the right direction," Savell explains. "We resist trying to drive BPR and instead concentrate on being consultants because the only way BPR will work is for management to put it consistently in front. So far, they've been willing to make that effort. Time will tell, but we're very pleased so far," he concludes.

A
Case Study
by
John McCloud

McDonnell Douglas Transport Aircraft

In late 1991, McDonnell Douglas Transport Aircraft, a unit of McDonnell Douglas Corporation in Long Beach, Calif., inaugurated a reengineering program for the assembly of the C-17 military cargo plane. Based on a protocol known as process variability reduction (PVR), the program is intended to make improvements in the assembly process that both shorten the time required to put one of the aircraft together and reduce the number of defects and mistakes in the final product. The stated goals are to:

- develop schedule and program predictability;
- assure product performance; and
- maintain (contractual) cost compliance.

The program initially targeted three components of the assembly process: the portion of wingspan assembly that involves the use of Drivmatic riveting machines; pylon stub assembly; and fuel system assembly, with the objective of eliminating fuel leaks. The company organized three separate teams to institute change in each of the targeted processes, staggering introduction of the new approach over the first half of 1992.

The Drivmatics team was chosen to go first, developing procedures and techniques that would subsequently be adopted — and adapted — by the two later teams. By summer of 1993, the Drivmatic team's work had progressed through a complete cycle and produced very dramatic results: a 75 percent drop in work time on assembly of the wing skin for a single shipset (i.e., two wings), from

21,529 hours in January 1992 to 5,254 hours in July 1993 (see figure 1). Moreover, the portion of those totals that represented time spent correcting mistakes experienced especially spectacular declines, plunging from 8,625 hours at the beginning to a mere 611 hours 16 months later. The company estimates cost savings of $1 million per plane from this procedure alone.

The pylon stub and fuel system teams appear to be heading for equally impressive results, and the company has enlarged the scope of its PVR efforts to encompass 16 distinct components, including two that deal with paperwork related to the C-17 rather than mechanical processes and three that entail participation by outside suppliers, who are being encouraged to implement their own PVR programs based on MDA-developed patterns.

Transport aircraft unit overview
Over the past few years, the McDonnell Douglas Corp. has significantly reorganized its corporate structure, closing down some divisions and creating new companies with greater independence. As part of this process, the corporation has rearranged units into more coherent and pragmatic groupings designed to be able to compete for a broader array of public and private contracts.

In August 1992, the Transport Aircraft unit, which is based in a 1.1 million-square-foot main assembly facility and a 650,000 square-foot sub-assembly facility adjacent to the Long Beach Airport, was shifted from the Douglas Aircraft Co. to McDonnell Douglas Aerospace, (MDA), a new government-oriented aerospace group. Included in the new regional division were the former McDonnell Douglas Space Systems Co. and McDonnell Douglas Electronics Systems Co. Organizational changes were made in Transport Aircraft to align with the new operational structure.

Employment structure — The Transport Aircraft unit has close to 12,000 employees. About 10,000 of them work in the above facilities near the McDonnell Douglas Corp. headquarters and a warehouse three miles away in the city of Carson. About 500 employees handle some sub-assembly duties at a company facility in Macon, Ga., and the remainder fabricate parts for both the C-17 and commercial liners at a government-owned plant in Columbus, Ohio. The last facility is being phased out.

The employees of Transport Aircraft represent the entire spectrum of the aerospace industry, including shop-floor mechanics, buyers, logistic specialists, contract administrators and Ph.D.-level

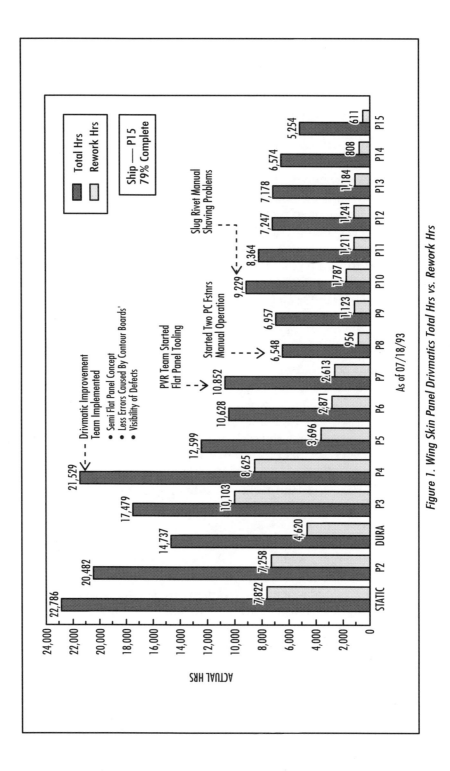

Figure 1. Wing Skin Panel Drivmatics Total Hrs vs. Rework Hrs

engineers and scientists. Four levels of management exist between the senior vice president in charge and the nonmanagement employee. Some engineering personnel are members of a professional association that acts as a bargaining unit. The majority of production employees are represented by the United Aerospace Workers (UAW) union, Local 142. The UAW's bargaining unit and seniority lists cover both Transport Aircraft and Douglas Aircraft Co.; consequently changes in employment needs in one segment may affect employees in the other segment.

Product—Transport Aircraft has one major product—the C-17 airlift aircraft, a four-engine jet transport being built for the U.S. Air Force. The unit is under contract for the aircraft's design, development, production, flight testing and deployment support. Unlike existing airlift aircraft, the C-17 can transport large combat or disaster-relief equipment, carry heavy loads over intercontinental distances and land at small airfields. It has low maintenance needs and low life-cycle costs, an important factor in an era of declining defense budgets.

Apart from its work on the C-17, the unit has several other functions. These are: providing logistics support (including spare parts, sustaining engineering and technical publications) for the Air Force's KC-10 tanker cargo aircraft; conducting research for the Air Force, Navy and NASA; managing programs involving the military use of Douglas commercial aircraft, including a program to modify the DC-10 to serve as tanker cargo aircraft for the Royal Netherlands Air Force; and performing independent research and development and providing research and technical support for commercial airliner programs of Douglas Aircraft Co.. Additional subassembly work for commercial airliners is being phased out.

Customer— The principal contracting agency for the C-17 is the System Program Office (SPO) of Air Force Material Command, which maintains day-to-day contact with the unit. However, a range of other military and federal government offices have both an interest in and influence over the program and contract. Among these are: the Program Executive Officer for Tactical and Airlift Programs in the Office of the Assistant Secretary of the Air Force for Acquisition; the Assistant Secretary of Defense for Acquisition in the Department of Defense, which also plays a role in the purchase of the aircraft; and four committees in the U.S. Congress that exercise authorization and appropriations authority in the purchase of the C-17.

In addition, the eventual end-user of the product, the Air

Force Air Mobility Command, plays a vital oversight role in the aircraft's development, production, and logistic support arrangements in order to ensure that the craft meets the needs of the command's mission. Furthermore, as prime customers of AMC airlift services, the U.S. Army and U.S. Marine Corps had significant input in setting C-17 requirements and actively participate in operational testing and evaluation of the aircraft.

The Defense Contract Management Command disburses payments and, through the Defense Plant Representative Office (DPRO), administers the contract and ensures compliance with all appropriate government regulations. The Defense Contract Audit Agency performs audits of current contracts as well as proposals for follow-on contracts. The Government Accounting Office, the investigative arm of Congress, has representatives on site to report on program status.

All these entities together comprise the overall customer and are part of the customer focus that must be maintained by the program. The complex network of players creates an exceptionally intricate review structure that complicates the C-17 assembly process and makes the accomplishment of improvements in that process all the more difficult.

History of the C-17 program
The C-17 program arose in reaction to the Iran hostage crisis, where it became apparent that the nation's Rapid Deployment Force lacked sufficient mobility to respond expeditiously to emergencies in remote locations. The Pentagon issued a request for development proposals for a new airlifter in late 1980, and in August 1981, McDonnell Douglas was awarded the contract. However, Congress withheld funding for the program for more than a year, and then earmarked only $30 million for research, an amount most experts considered inadequate.

Continuing funding disputes, numerous requests for design changes and changing military goals have burdened the program throughout its brief history, making it difficult to proceed in a timely and efficient manner. The program did not enter full-scale engineering and development until 1985. The initial program called for 210 aircraft and a maximum production rate of 29 aircraft per year. But the initial purchase agreements by Congress fell well short of the original program plans. In 1988 Congress authorized purchase of the first two aircraft, following up a year later with a call for only four more.

Since that time, the planning environment for the C-17 has remained unstable. For example, in 1990, Congress again authorized only four aircraft, despite the fact that a program evaluation had determined that six was the minimum necessary to maintain an orderly and cost-efficient buildup of the production rate.

Also in 1990, after a review of major aircraft programs in light of the changing world situation, the Secretary of Defense cut the planned program from 210 to 120 aircraft and lowered the annual peak production rate to an unspecified level below the 29 initially intended. Congress provided no C-17 acquisition funding for fiscal year 1991, forcing a restructuring of the contract and amendments to the delivery schedule. For 1992, Congress authorized acquisition of four aircraft, again two below the planned level.

The first C-17 flew Sept. 15, 1991, a full decade after McDonnell Douglas won the contract. A year later, four aircraft participated in the flight-test program and two other nonflying airframes were run in a ground-test program. With the C-17 program nearing the end of its development and initial production phase, the first non-test aircraft was delivered to the U.S. Air Mobility Command at Charleston Air Force Base, S.C., in 1993.

Restructuring program background

Shortly after the C-17's maiden flight, MDA executives met with SPO and DPRO representatives to discuss continuing problems with cost and scheduling overruns in the airship's assembly. Both sides agreed the problems needed serious attention. According to Ron Mertz, an MDA senior technical specialist who was the program's initial PVR manager, the company had managed to meet the contracted delivery schedule but only by delivering planes that had to be returned for several thousand hours of reworking.

For the military, timeliness and quality control were the overriding issues. SPO warned that if MDA could not correct the deficiencies, the company would lose the contract. According to both MDA and SPO representatives, the warning was not so much adversarial as instructive. The Air Force wanted the program to proceed and offered to help MDA solve its problems.

Shel Hess, who succeeded Mertz as senior manager over PVR, candidly acknowledges that the easy relationship that had developed between the military and its contractors up through the early 1980s had allowed companies to become lax. The government typically covered military cost overruns with few questions asked.

"We had little incentive to improve our procedures," he points out.

But with the C-17, the pattern changed. The C-17 program originated, and remains, under a fixed-price development contract. The government instituted this type of contract in response to public outrage over revelations of $2,000 toilet seats, $400 wrenches and other apparently extreme expenditures by the Pentagon. To counteract its spendthrift image, the Department of Defense began using fixed-price contracts in the mid-1980s. Although the Pentagon has since discontinued use of these arrangements, deeming them generally unworkable, the original C-17 contract remains in place. The C-17 is, in fact, the only major fixed-contract DoD program still in operation.

Under the contract's conditions, no matter how much time the Air Transport unit spends on putting a plane together, the payment to MDA remains largely unchanged. Although the company does receive some adjustments for program alterations made at the government's request, the adjustments do not necessarily cover all the extra costs. And, unlike the past when the Pentagon typically covered suppliers' cost overruns, under the C-17 contract, MDA has to pay for its own delays and mistakes out of pocket.

Thus, MDA had a double incentive to improve the C-17's level of conformance to stipulated standards. Refusal to take meaningful steps toward revamping its quality control system could mean loss of the entire contract (and likely shutdown of the facility); and even if that scenario did not materialize, cost overruns would put the company in the red, possibly forcing it to terminate involvement in the program on its own.

Process variability reduction protocol

To correct the deficiencies, MDA agreed to introduce a reengineering program for the C-17 assembly, bringing together employees from various McDonnell Douglas divisions to form a program development and implementation task force. David Braunstein, a specialist in quality control who had at one time worked for NASA, was selected as director of what was termed C-17 process integration. Jim Arnold, a manufacturing systems engineer and civilian employee, represented SPO on the panel. Jerry Guardado represented DPRO.

SPO had been working with military suppliers to improve their performance since the mid 1980s, basing its efforts on an Air Force document known as "Reliability and Maintainability 2000," or

RM 2000. The purpose of the document, according to Arnold, is to guide military suppliers toward establishment of manufacturing processes by the year 2000 that guarantee superior-performing products at lower overall cost.

Arnold says RM 2000 focuses on development of effective protocols that are appropriate to the individual company and to the product(s) involved. "It is not a blueprint of how to do it," he emphasizes. Rather, it offers a guiding philosophy and suggestions on approaches to instituting quality improvement programs.

For the C-17 effort, MDA opted to work within the criteria used for the Malcolm Baldrige National Quality Award, and the MDA-SPO team ultimately settled on a Process Variability Reduction protocol developed by SPO. Adoption of the protocol was written into the contract, with extra money added to finance establishment of the program.

The PVR concept, Hess explains, is simple: If you adequately control the process, you do not need to worry about the product. Through PVR, a producer attempts to maintain the results of repeated tasks within specified parameters by reducing the opportunities for mechanical or human error.

PVR works by determining an ideal and measurable standard of performance for every task, establishing an allowable range of deviation from the norm, then figuring out the means to achieve the desired results. These means can include — but are not limited to — product or parts redesign/reengineering, equipment modification or replacement, introduction of more accurate measuring devices and techniques, worker retraining or reassignment, and revising the line of command. Effective use of the methodology requires procedures and equipment that allow workers to quickly, accurately and easily assess their individual conformance to a given standard as they work, rather than relying primarily on external auditing after the work is complete.

Targeted functions

As the first stage in PVR implementation, the development team broke the C-17 assembly process into two dozen sub-task areas. It then identified the eight that seemed to be producing the most problems. Finally, it selected three target areas to become pilot programs for PVR implementation.

According to John Gaffney, an industrial technologist for MDA, the team selected the three pilot areas on the basis of:

- high visibility, problems that were giving the client the most concern or that had the highest percentage of obvious mistakes;
- quick turnaround, problems where tangible improvements could be attained in a relatively short time; and
- significant payback, problems that when corrected would have the largest impact on overall product improvement and would produce the greatest fiscal benefit.

The pilot programs selected involved use of the Drivmatic machine in wing skin assembly, pylon stub assembly and detection and prevention of fuel leaks. The last, Gaffney reports, is a problem for all heavy cargo and many high-velocity planes, not necessarily a shortcoming of the MDA assembly process; but solving it for the C-17 presumably could lead to eliminating or reducing fuel leakage in other aircraft as well.

The Drivmatic example

The first area to begin PVR implementation was the Drivmatic unit. Gaffney, who was selected to head up the PVR steering team for this unit, reports that McDonnell Douglas has used Drivmatic machines for about 30 years. It is a common piece of equipment in the industry. The C-17 wing assembly unit currently uses five G-1700 models developed especially for MDA by GemCorp of Buffalo, N.Y.

The Drivmatic might best be described as the modern-day equivalent of Rosie the Riveter, except that it too requires its Rosie (or Roger) to operate it. But unlike the recognizable handtool of the '40s, the Drivmatic weighs close to a ton and is more akin to a cargo lift than a typical electric drill. The operator sits at the controls and moves the machine along the wingspan, which at this point has not been attached to the plane.

The machine has two functions. First it drills a hole in the wing skin, then it secures a fastener in that hole. Standard Drivmatics work by means of forced upset: an indexed head slug fastener is installed in a hole whose diameter matches that of the fastener; then the machine pushes it upward until the fastener is forged in place.

By contrast, the G-1700 operates by means of a "coldworking" procedure. The G-1700 begins by drilling a dual diameter hole, with the opening set to match the diameter of the slug and the center set to a reduced dimension. A pin is pushed in, then squeezed from both sides until it expands to lock into the hole, simultaneously forcing expansion of the narrower part of the hole. In some cases, two pins, each of a different metal or alloy, are inserted from opposite ends, then forged together by the same squeezing action. Finally, the Drivmatic shaves any excess material from the pin that remains on the surface until it is flush to a maximum height of .002 inch.

The G-1700 method, which increases the strength of both the rivet and the overall wing, requires up to 40,000 pounds of force per insertion. Completion of a full wingset takes approximately 44,000 Drivmatic repetitions.

According to Gaffney, the Drivmatic process had several shortcomings. First, the machine did not always shave the pins closely enough, resulting in the need for operators to complete the shaving process by hand and slowing down assembly. This problem was complicated by the fact that the gauges used to measure excess pin height depended upon visual readings by the operator or auditor. Measurements were thus subject to great variability in their accuracy. Because excessive pin height could cause flight drag that limits the aircraft's fuel load, inaccurate readings could significantly undermine the C-17's performance.

The Drivmatic procedure also produced mounding, excess expansion that raised the metal surrounding the fastener. That, too, could produce drag, though no one knew to what extent. In addition, the Drivmatic sometimes improperly installed the two-piece fasteners, leaving a weak forge that could have very serious consequences during flight.

Further complications arose from the fact that individual machines seemed to perform at differing levels of reliability. The work of some operators also was better than that of others, not to mention better at some times than at others. Predictability and repeatability were low.

The overall process created frequent delays, delays that were compounded by the need to test the machine's performance at frequent intervals by producing "coupons," examples of each Drivmatic's output on non-wingskin blocks, to determine how well it was performing. Yet more delay was caused by the need for thorough checks of the final product by designated auditors. And perhaps the greatest delay of all was the time spent redoing work that had already been done when an auditor found errors.

Beginning implementation

Implementation of PVR in the Drivmatics process began Jan. 14, 1992. Getting it started was no easy task. Not only did a total strategy and plan have to be devised, a working team created and problems clearly identified, but an entire department had to be convinced to alter its accustomed way of doing things and begin to work as a team. That the Air Transport unit consisted heavily of relatively new hires who had joined the company since 1988 made this less a problem than it might have been. Nevertheless, employees had been there long enough to have adopted a comfortable routine, and many had enough experience in corporate industry to have developed a mistrust of, if not outright antagonism toward, management.

The commencement of job cutbacks in McDonnell Douglas commercial divisions around the same time put many employees on guard. To them, restructuring was likely to mean only one thing — layoffs for some and an increased workload for the rest.

Mike McCrabb, senior manager for the wing panel and spans department who ended up with the task of adapting the generalized PVR plan to his department's specific operations, confesses he was one of those who held that view.

"I resisted the change because I anticipated extra work," he says. "I feared it." On the other hand, he adds, "I knew we were in trouble and needed help, so I was willing to reach for anything I could grab."

Although he expected resistance from others as well, McCrabb recognized that the employees in his unit were eager for some kind of change. Problems identified by workers on the floor often went unreported to foremen or managers because of a history of non-response.

"There's nothing more frustrating for mechanics on the floor than to know things aren't working right but nobody's doing anything about it," he remarks. Consequently, if a problem came up, the floor workers simply looked for a way to fix it at the point where it showed up rather than attempting to trace it back to its origin."

"I always wondered why we never really got things fixed in the factory," says Braunstein. "The reason was we never went after every single factor that contributed to the problem. People went after short-term solutions that didn't get to the root of what was wrong."

Braunstein himself suffered from the same tendency. As he relates, "When we got going, one of the questions that kept coming up was how important keeping the head heights within the .002-inch limit really was. We went to the Air Force and argued that it didn't make that much difference. I naively thought that making the requirement easier was all we needed to do. I was wrong. The problems were much deeper than that."

A determination to correct deficiencies from the root up meant that the initial stages of implementation became, in Braunstein's words, "one of the biggest detective stories I've ever seen. We had to scour the whole process to learn how everything fit together and where the problem areas lay."

Setting PVR in motion

As the unit's designated process improvement manager, Gaffney had the responsibility of introducing the wingspan unit to the concept of PVR and, with the cooperation of management and floor workers, creating a unit steering team.

The wingspan steering team, which had the task of modifying the PVR protocol to fit the unit's work and continues to have responsibility for its effective application, consists of 14 members. Eight came from either the wingspan unit itself or from other assembly units that had direct involvement with wingspan output. For example, there were two quality engineers and one member from quality assurance. SPO and DPRO had two members each, though their participation was limited. In addition to McCrabb, unit members included the Drivmatic production manager, a portable and perishable tooling specialist and two maintenance and facilities employees. Gaffney and aeronautical engineer John Braun were the two PVR planning team representatives.

Two other standing teams — statistical process control and proof of process — were also created, with representatives from the steering committee and additional floor reps. Each of the three teams meets for one hour a week during the standard work day. Additional meetings are held with assembly workers to keep them abreast of developments, give them training or instruction, answer questions they have about changes and responsibilities and get their feedback.

Not officially on the team but a major contributor to the process was industrial engineer Shirvin Sarkosh. Sarkosh performed much of the statistical tracking of such things as employee hours per wingset and number of fasteners installed per hour, performed cost analyses, and assessed machine modification requirements. He also contributed to task analysis and task field observation.

Under Braunstein's supervision, Gaffney stressed employee participation in the PVR effort from the outset, beginning with selection of members of the wingspan unit's PVR team.

Using Gaffney's term, the wingspan department would "own"

the specific PVR protocol it developed. "The process owner has to be involved," he insists. "We believe that having someone from outside come in and dictate what changes will be made is a mistake."

Gaffney even considers himself and other representatives from the overall PVR planning team to be outsiders to a large extent. Their role, he says, is to explain the PVR concept, show what kind of tools are available to implement the protocol and help train unit workers in their use. Their function was neither to hand over a ready-made program nor to create one while the unit looked on. They serve, rather, as guides and advisors.

According to Braunstein, transforming the standard PVR protocol into one tailored by and for the specific user increases the likelihood that the process will "take" — that the affected workforce will assimilate the components, put them into practice and continue to maintain and refine the process over time.

McCrabb concurs, saying, "If someone were to impose responsibilities on the unit, there would be more resentment, resistance and less sense of ownership."

Part of the rewritten contract with SPO mandated the introduction of new analytical tools to the C-17 assembly. Among the ones Gaffney brought to the effort encompass a wide variety of analytic, statistical and organizational methodologies, as well as flow charts, P-charts, fishbone charts, intricate project timetables and innovative task measurement techniques (see figure 2). Many of these are tools are based on work by top U.S. and Japanese business process theoreticians. Their underlying purpose is to train unit workers to take a more analytic approach to their jobs and to provide them with a tangible framework in which to do this.

Since most steering team members who come from the assembly floor do not have four-year college degrees, much of this initially seemed, says McCrabb, like gobbledygook. Yet today, McCrabb, who worked his way up the ranks, is completely comfortable both discussing and employing sampling size, tolerance, deviation from the norm, CP and CPK standards and other complex analytic procedures and terms.

The analysis of the assembly process turned up many opportunities for improvement. Among the most useful changes were the introduction of detailed performance charts; identification of every step of the assembly process, analysis of its defects and potential for positive adjustments, and establishment of definable short- and long-term goals; and improvement task timetables with clear target dates.

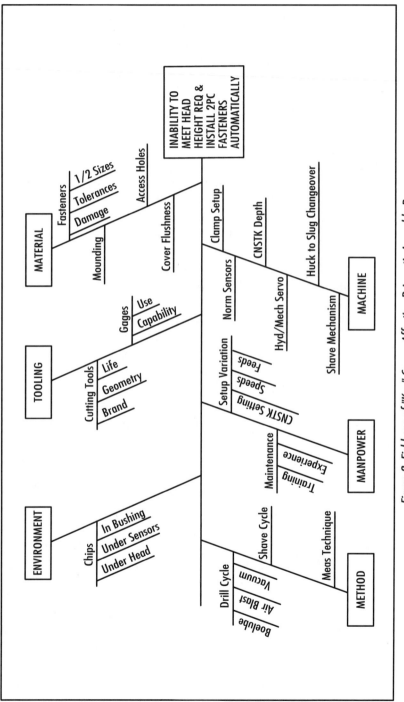

Figure 2. Fishbone of "Key" Causes Affecting Drivmatic Assembly Processes

Implementation of one measure often revealed the need for additional ones that had not previously been considered. For example, the attempt to chart the accuracy of the Drivmatics' performance was hampered by the dependence on mechanics' visual reports using difficult-to-read gauges. Recognition of this shortcoming lead to the purchase of digital gauges that not only performed consistently but also gave clear and virtually unmistakable readouts. The digital gauges had the added value of requiring less time to use, saving yet more time and producing a better result.

The use of digital gauges in turn opened still more opportunities for increasing efficiency. A plan is now in the works to mount the gauges directly on the Drivmatics and link them to a computer running the Genesis program. This will mean continuous and automatic measurement that can be instantly analyzed, with rapid feedback to both the operator and the tracking team. Variability problems will be detected almost instantaneously before the machine has the chance to make numerous repetitions of the error.

On the other hand, better gauging revealed that the Drivmatics were not capable of achieving the desired level of accuracy over an extended period, necessitating modifications to the machines themselves. Completion of those modifications, however, led to a better product. The team is now working on additional modifications that will enable the Drivmatics to handle the approximately 8,000 non-pin fasteners that currently have to be installed by operators using hand-held pneumatic devices.

Impact of PVR

McCrabb's fear that PVR would mean more work turned out to be true. In his case, the weekly meetings and the time spent learning how to use the charts and analytic methodologies sometimes left him frazzled. At the same time, he says, the new ideas, new responsibilities and measurable signs of product improvement were energizing.

Additional responsibilities were also placed on floor workers from the beginning, with a request to provide detailed inventories of their job tasks, tools and procedures. New chains of command were established, with individual work groups formed into more coherent teams complete with designated leaders whose duties included conveying information and training back and forth between the floor teams and the PVR standing teams. Although as anticipated, some employees initially resisted change, over time most came to embrace the new process and take pride in the results.

New responsibilities continue to be added. They come in various forms but stem from problems identified in the detailed analysis of the wing assembly process. For example, preventative maintenance on the Drivmatics, which used to be performed once a year, is now done weekly since it was ultimately recognized that the machines' breakdown rate could be significantly reduced by frequent corrective actions.

As noted above, the Drivmatic machines required modification to perform their tasks more accurately and efficiently. Jim Mecklenburg, the portable and perishable tooling representative on the unit's PVR steering team, found his job expanding from routine troubleshooting on the floor to helping solve this and other problems. Working with the mechanics, he put together a description of the needed modifications, then shopped it around different vendors.

Demonstrating how the teamwork concept has caught on, one of the vendors bidding for the Drivmatics modification contract was the machines' manufacturer, GemCorp. The floor mechanics were asked to make their recommendation, and they unanimously rejected all bids, including GemCorp's, arguing they were too high. Mecklenburg, who continues to serve as a liaison with outside vendors on various PVR-related projects, resumed scouting and eventually found a local source that offered to do the modification for less than one tenth of other bids. The resulting work met all the performance standards MDA had requested in the contract.

"We treat our mechanics as assets rather than liabilities, people who are there to help us," reports McCrabb. "They have increased responsibility for their individual output, which is more stressful, but it also gives them a greater feeling of achievement. They recognize that what they do counts."

By almost any kind of measure, the introduction of PVR into the wingspan unit can only be judged a success. Both the total number of employee hours per wingset and the number of rework hours continue to decline about 10 percent every six weeks. The unit dramatically reduced the number of fastenings that fall outside the contracted range of acceptability and has gradually compressed that range. There has been no reduction in the workforce and, despite the added responsibilities, the amount of overtime has fallen significantly.

"It's quickly going from a formal process that you have to concentrate on to a natural way of doing business," says McCrabb.

Beyond Drivmatics

Following the success of the three pilot programs, the planning team completed plans for 13 additional process improvement projects, six of which are in some stage of implementation. As the last of the projects move to the implementation stage, says Braunstein, the task force will move to the next level of improvement. And then to the next, in a continuous cycle of refinement.

According to Hess, the PVR planning team has grown to 21 members and will soon grow to 28. Although most of the initial team members came from within the company, subsequent hiring efforts included looking to outside sources for people with substantial experience in process reengineering and quality control in a manufacturing environment.

It takes a team four to six months to write an individual plan and another four or five months to get implementation established. Braunstein says they have developed four organizational methodologies that form the framework for each plan. The methodologies cover:

- how to pick a problem;
- how to fix it once identified;
- how to institutionalize the process so the problem doesn't recur; and
- how to capture the gains economically.

The first and fourth are particularly important, Braunstein stresses, adding, "We get involved in issues that are the most complex."

Each potential PVR target project has to go through two filters. The first filter determines whether the problem is sufficiently complex and requires a dedicated team to address it. The second examines the return on investment in terms of the seriousness of identified defects, the length of time required to implement and the cost. Making an informed decision, he notes, requires information from workers on the floor, input from the industrial engineering department, feedback from the customer and results from flight tests.

As for capturing economic gains, Braunstein comments, "A favorite phrase among process improvement experts is 'cost avoidance.' It's not enough to avoid costs. You also have to produce savings. For example, the Air Force is into buying airplanes that cost less, less and less. We're interested in being more competitive, which means we have to produce at costs that are less, less and less."

PVR limitations

Although everyone involved with the C-17 effort expresses satisfaction with the process improvement effort, they all agree that the C-17 program was not the perfect situation in which to try out a PVR protocol.

"Although PVR can be applied in any kind of manufacturing environment, airframe assembly is one of the hardest places to implement it," explains Arnold. "It was first envisioned for electronics, and it benefits from the kind of high productivity you have there. The more often you repeat the process, the more improvement you can expect to achieve."

The two-plane and four-plane a year cycles that have been typical of the C-17 program, he says, fail to exploit PVR's full potential. On the other hand, he adds, "We're very happy with the way things worked out. Drivmatics is our best effort so far, even if theoretically it's not the optimum PVR environment."

Ideally, say those involved, PVR should be implemented at the inception of a project and applied to every facet of manufacture and assembly. In the case of the C-17, that was not possible. Design was complete and production well under way by the time the protocol was introduced. In addition, MDA instituted PVR in the assembly plant only, not at the manufacturing end (though the Air Transport unit has recently exported the program to the manufacturers of a few key components). The drawback to this partial approach is that lack of quality control at the manufacturing end tends to undermine efforts to improve the assembly process by supplying defective parts or providing delayed or incomplete delivery.

Nonetheless, both the MDA and SPO representatives agree that whatever the shortcomings of any particular approach, the implementation or process improvement protocol is worth the effort. Once a protocol is in place, it promotes continuous improvement. There is no definite end-point. With the C-17 assembly, for example, when the product of any sub-assembly area consistently falls within its targeted range of deviation, the target range is contracted.

Or as Hess puts it, "No matter how good you get, it pays to get better."

A
Case Study
by
Brad Bambarger

Mellon Bank Corp.

Fraught with change, the defined-contribution business presents opportunities only for those financial institutions that can meet the challenge of radically escalated customer expectations. Once satisfied with cyclical valuation and the attendant monthly statements, the 401(k) retirement plan market now demands daily valuations with instantaneous updates and service. Mellon Bank Corp.'s Master Trust Services is meeting this challenge by transforming the way it conducts business, using sophisticated technology to reengineer its information systems and workflow management.

In its 125th year of operation, the Pittsburgh, Pa.-based Mellon Bank Corp. is one of the nation's leading financial institutions, with 1993 net income of $420 million. Mellon's fee-based services — trust and investment, cash management, mortgage banking and securities transfer — are particularly productive, with the trust division administering about $750 billion in assets (see figure 1). Going where the money is, Mellon has ventured increasingly into these fee-based businesses, recently acquiring The Boston Co. for approximately $1.5 billion and, pending regulatory approval, purchasing The Dreyfus Corp. for nearly $1.9 billion.

The Society of Professional Administrators and Recordkeepers (SPAR) estimates that as of year-end 1992 the U.S. pension market accounted for $3.59 trillion in assets. So, of course, it is not only Mellon Bank vying for a greater share of that pie. Mutual fund companies are gaining on banks' market share in this arena. According to SPAR, banks' share of the defined-contribution market had declined by year-end 1992 to 31 percent from 37 percent in 1987. In the same period, mutual fund companies had doubled their share of the industry, to 18 percent from 9 percent. In the 401(k) market specifically, competition has become even tighter. By year-end 1992, mutual fund companies had narrowed the market share gap with banks to 3 percent.

In this accelerating race to satisfy a more sophisticated, demanding customer pool and gain an edge in a growing, lucrative market, Mellon Trust has designed an ambitious business process reengineering (BPR) plan that banks on technological investment and forward-minded methodologies as competitive advantages. But using technology to improve business processes is nothing new to Mellon. *Computer World* magazine rated Mellon Bank No. 2 among the nation's financial services firms as part of its 1993 ranking of the most effective organizations in managing and utilizing information technology. What is new to the Mellon Trust initiative is that it is part of a major reengineering effort supported by the division's Business Performance Improvement department.

As vice president in charge of Business Performance Improvement, Don Barber coordinates the BPR project for Mellon Trust's 401(k) program. With the strategic leadership of Tim Keaney, senior vice president of retirement services, and the technical input of an outside consulting firm specializing in systems development and office automation, Barber and his team have put together a program that aims to revolutionize the way Mellon Trust processes and services 401(k) accounts. The program's goal is to have marketing strategies and financial controls dictate operational systems, not the other way around. Its approach is to reorganize the 401(k) department, interfacing the old mainframe "legacy" systems with an integrated, PC-based, flexible operation aligned with the tenets of technical innovation and continuous improvement.

Adapting to a changing market

As the working population ages, the more it becomes interested in the details of its retirement plans. Employees take advantage of 401(k) plans to use pre- and post-tax money to save for retirement, with taxes on earnings deferred until withdrawal. These plans generally offer various investment choices, from money market accounts to international stock funds. With the increased interest in such plans comes the demand for increased service and information access. "Plan participants have become an awfully lot more enlightened," explains Keaney.

"They're recognizing that 401(k) plans and the valuable assets that they're putting into them will become increasingly important as questions arise regarding the funding status of social security, the funding of defined-benefit programs, and the merger and acquisition activity going on in the corporate world."

Participants also have become more aware, Keaney says, that "in a 401(k) plan the participant controls the investment dollars, not the person's company or another third party. Participants are now demanding from service providers like Mellon the technology that allows them to more easily and accurately control their financial destiny."

Valuing 401(k) plans daily requires the latest in record-keeping and voice-response technology, which helps provide plan participants with 24-hour access to up-to-date investment information. With this data, participants can make informed decisions, tracking their holdings and transferring funds should their investment objectives require it. Such ease of use and increased awareness help promote employee satisfaction and foster greater participation in a company's 401(k) plan.

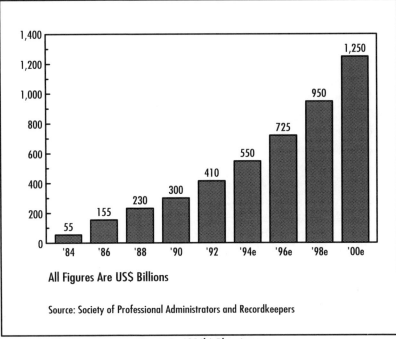

All Figures Are US$ Billions

Source: Society of Professional Administrators and Recordkeepers

Figure 1. 401(k) Plan Assets

Previously, the Mellon Trust defined-contribution department operated on a defined-benefit philosophy, revolving around monthly processing. But even with the monthly lead time, the operational components of cash management, reconciling Mellon record keeping with client payroll, and working in an automated manner with outside fund managers presented challenges to outmoded technology and workflow management. Up to 50 percent of a trust employee's time had been consumed by nonvalue-added activities, such as typing, photocopying and coordinating information that is not universally disseminated.

With this old system, trust employees were forced to concentrate on the process rather than the customer. Up to six copies of a document had to be produced and distributed between several different floors in two separate buildings. This constant passing of data back and forth not only took up valuable time but created a propensity for potential errors. And these procedures were also less responsive. Client service was slowed due to the mountains of paper to sift, work standardization was difficult to achieve, and statistical compilation was conducted manually. "Reports on service quality took two months to prepare [on the monthly system]," says Barber. "So on April 1, you're reporting February 1 results. By then, the numbers aren't of much use because things have changed. It's like expecting quality checks to come at the end of the line in an auto plant — by then, it's too late."

"Monthly processing was a disintegrated process that could exist because of the less intense workflow," Keaney adds. "At the end of each month, we had 15 to 20 days to reconcile account balances and begin production of customer statements. Today, customers want the ability to call us through an 800 number and get today's balances and input transactions via the telephone. They want to talk to a trained, knowledgeable individual who has access to the total history of their relationship and can effect any transaction that a 401(k) plan participant would want."

Historically, the human resource (HR) departments of the client companies administered 401(k) plans. With downsizing so prevalent, many HR departments cannot provide this service anymore and must outsource. With the new system, Mellon can offer a turnkey service to clients, freeing HR departments to pursue other duties. The new plan administration area will feature a telephone center with an 800 number to handle requests for loan applications, questions about interest rates, changes to withholding amounts, etc.

Plan administration also will take care of paperwork fulfillment as well as provide an employee communications group that will be available to go on-site to explain the 401(k) plan to participants.

"A 401(k) plan is a benefit," Barber says, "and no company wants a benefit administered sloppily. So a company should be able to call us to hear their employees' feedback regarding this benefit, to see the types of calls that have been registered. Our quality program had been manually driven, but now we will be able to keep statistics on quality on a real-time basis, categorizing calls *automatically*. How many address changes? Application requests? Complaints? This reporting capability is necessary because we're transparent to the participant; complaints reflect on the client company, not Mellon Bank. So clients, understandably, want it tightly run . . . I see [the new system] as night and day in terms of responsiveness and the level of service we can provide."

Mellon Trust's workflow management system

Enlisting the expertise of an outside consultant enabled Mellon Trust to verify its BPR concepts as sound and determine that the concepts were economically feasible, says Barber (see figure 2). The consultant also developed a demonstration system for Mellon employees "like a little lab room," Barber adds. This system simulation was not only an excellent tool for orienting employees but for marketing as well. Potential clients were shown the system to exhibit Mellon's dedication to improving service quality.

According to Keaney, outside consultants are helpful in validating the assumptions and conclusions of proposed reengineering plans. Also, he says, outside experts tend to be much more on the cutting edge of the BPR tools and technology Mellon Trust requires: computer hardware and software, workflow management systems, relational databases, electronic mail and messaging. "With technology changing so rapidly, it's nice to be able to rely on someone who is up-to-date on all the tools we need," Keaney says. "Technology has really changed the competitive landscape. When we come to the table with specific ideas for reengineering, outside firms have been instrumental in helping us with the technical means to accomplish those tasks."

Mellon describes the new workflow management system as an "intelligent" system that automatically, electronically manages and coordinates information associated with each step of the 401(k) process and each related department (plan administration, record

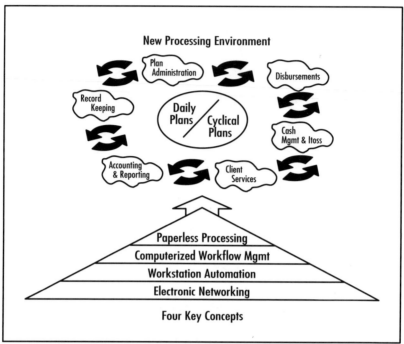

Figure 2. Four Key Concepts Drive New Processing Environment

keeping, accounting/reporting, client services, cash management and disbursement). Based on architecture consisting of an image server, PC workstations and local area networks (LAN), the system uses digital imaging to capture and display on workstations images of physical documents such as letters, forms and faxes. The system allows processing to be done at individual workstations while providing access to multiple mainframe systems and databases, and it is designed to facilitate report management by replacing paper or microfiche reports with computerized output to laser disk.

With this new system, each department captures and stores incoming client faxes directly into the system via fax modem. Documents received through the mail will be scanned into the system manually. A plan administrator reviews each image at his or her workstation to determine what action the account requires, entering the appropriate process codes and related information. The system then creates an electronic file "folder" and routes it to the appropriate departments via the LAN for further processing. The system audits each electronic file folder, and if any information is missing or incorrect, the system allows the plan administrator to write a brief note that is either automatically faxed back to the client or input into an automatic "call back" reminder. Once one activity in the service process is complete, the person responsible for the next step sees it queued on his or her workstation along with processing instructions. Each workstation automatically interfaces with all mainframe processing systems so that it eliminates the effort of logging-on and accessing multiple systems, as well as the need to constantly re-enter data such as account name and number.

Keaney and Barber expect this new system to yield benefits in four areas:

Quality — The new system should:
• reduce errors due to a lack of information;
• immediately detect processing difficulties;
• facilitate employee training in how to avoid errors;
• eliminate rc-entry of data into multiple systems;
• build in work rules and error detection;
• automatically track and report service quality measures; and
• decrease risks associated with missed steps or misinterpretations of data.

Service — The new system should:
• easily accommodate customized service requests;
• produce accurate client status reports instantaneously;
• make management reports customized, more timely and more accurate;
• foster teamwork and client interaction;
• provide on-line responses to customer inquiries without delay;
• archive all documents and back-up notes in an electronic file folder; and
• automatically log all service inquiries.

Speed — The new system should:
• eliminate delays due to missing reminders or lack of follow-up;
• reduce work cycles with parallel processing;
• enable easier, quicker reallocation of staff resources to avoid backlogs;
• keep routine work flowing by eliminating time-consuming meetings and memos;
• implement revisions to processing requirements; and
• eliminate delays due to manual copying, logging and retrieving of files.

Control — The new system should:
* help enforce standard procedures;
* ensure that work files are accurate and up-to-date via a common workflow database;
* improve accountability by clearly defining which person is responsible for every step;
* automatically generate operating statistics for management review;
* automatically generate reminders and system checks;
* electronically create and seal audit trails; and
* guard against inadvertent or unwanted system disruptions through security controls.

From transactions to relationships

The new workflow management system will be rolled out over the next nine months. In this period, the BPR team will reclassify jobs and train staff on the new operating environment, as well as bring new clients onto the new system. Phase II of the reengineering will convert current monthly customers onto the new processing system. Because the new system's benefits also apply to cyclical valuation, customers who want to stay on the monthly plan will still profit. The monthly side is still a paper-intensive business, and centralized data collection, scanning and automatic routing have inherent benefits. "We think we can become much more cost-competitive," says Keaney.

Once the new system is in place, employees will receive technical training. Barber estimates that a telephone rep might need a week or two of training; client services people might require two to four half-day sessions. Even though the system has a user-friendly, icon-driven, Windows-like environment, it will require "a significant amount of training, even for casual users," Barber says. "You can have the best system in the world, but the people have to know how to use it to its potential."

But so far most of the training has been geared to orientation and cultural issues. Keaney and Barber held seven to 10 sessions of training with 401(k) department employees, with at most four to five people in each session. These sessions covered such topics as: What is reengineering? Why are we reengineering and why now? How does it affect you? What does it mean for the company?

"We talked about what a reengineering effort is all about and that, I think, defrayed a lot of concern people had over jobs changing or shuffling to different areas," Keaney says. "We said, 'We need to reengineer the process or else we'll be out of this business. And jobs may change as the process changes, but that will enable us to continue being a major player in the industry. And it's only through this kind of growth and the new business that comes from it that we can create opportunities for our people.'

"A positive by-product of this training was that it helped employees become less transaction-oriented and more customer-relationship-oriented," Keaney continues. "These sessions changed the concept of what a knowledgeable employee is. And that was uplifting for the entire organization. Just about everyone who has participated in the initial training understands that they play a particular role in the process and that if we were to only have 98 percent proficiency in all our process steps, we would probably only have about a 50 percent effectiveness rate overall. The awareness that 'I am a key link in the chain and have real input on customer satisfaction' is invaluable."

With all the changes facing Mellon in the past year, especially with the major acquisition of The Boston Co. and pending merger with Dreyfus, it has been difficult to find time to reengineer. According to Barber, "Managers are trying to run the day-to-day business while simultaneously gearing up for these acquisitions. Sometimes they say, 'Now's not the time. Don't come and talk to me about reengineering because I've got too much going on.' It's a tough decision to allocate resources to BPR when you need to conduct business as usual every day."

Customer demands = New opportunities

The reengineering of the 401(k) portion of Mellon's institutional trust area is a key project for Barber's Business Performance Improvement department. And though managers can turn to outside consulting firms rather than Barber's department for reengineering assistance, the project's success will surely invite entreaties from department heads in Mellon Trust's other areas: private asset management, jumbo mortgages, global securities, global asset management, investment services and investment products.

"Ours is clearly an effort that is being held up as a model within our institution," says Keaney. "I think that every three months [of the nine-month implementation period] we'll have qualitative and quantitative data on our progress. Teams are already being formulated to review the applicability of this new process and how well we incorporate technology with the 401(k) business so they can determine how it can be applied to other areas. This reengineering will have far-reaching implications for all our trust businesses."

The only negative so far, according to Keaney, has been the inevitable rub of self-examination. "When you really look inward and see how the functions are being performed, you see that maybe you're not doing things the best way you can do them. Analyzing yourself can be painful sometimes. You think, 'We should have gotten to some of these issues a lot sooner.' "

The fact that technology is changing so fast that many of the aforementioned technical innovations may eventually become obsolete doesn't concern Keaney — he takes it as a given. "It's the new methodology that will last, the new process that will stay," he says. "Going forward, we'll be able to match changing technology to this discipline. We'll be able to change easier to accommodate new customer needs quicker, as well as provide new products and services. So customer desires will become new opportunities for us. We think this is a healthy way for a company to be.

"We see a wheel of momentum coming. When you put the right infrastructure and the right product in place, you sell more business," Keaney adds. "When you sell more business, your organization grows. When your organization grows, then the jobs are changing, and there are career opportunities for our people. And everyone — our customers, our employees, our company — benefits. This process is really going to energize our organization."

A
Case Study
by
Brad Bambarger

OSRAM Sylvania

The standard-issue time cards used at an OSRAM Sylvania manufacturing plant in Pennsylvania were fine except they did not quite match the plant's time clock, which imprinted over the space designed for the employee's social security number. To process payroll, the numbers had to be legible, of course, so a diligent payroll clerk spent a few hours each week painstakingly recopying each employee's social security number onto a different space on the card. When the clerk went on vacation, a supervisor had to fill in for her, processing the time cards for payroll himself. Faced with hundreds of illegible social security numbers and a bad case of writer's cramp, the supervisor immediately called his office products supplier to order a more suitable type of time card, thereby freeing the clerk from considerable tedium and saving a bit of valuable time in the payroll process.

Though this example seems modest, it serves as a model for business process reengineering (BPR), illustrating that a key prerequisite to successful organizational change is the awareness that change is possible. The payroll clerk thought the ill-fitting time cards were an inescapable on-the-job irritation, so she was doing what she thought was the right thing — working harder. Fortunately, the supervisor knew that doing the best possible job did not necessarily mean working harder, but rather working smarter.

For a company to transform its business processes — whether simple administrative practices or complex manufacturing systems — it must not only chuck comfortable notions and conventional wisdom aside. It also has to discard drone mentalities and enlist the bright ideas of its employees, making them realize that change is not only possible — it is encouraged. Hoping such ideas illuminate its approach to BPR, OSRAM Sylvania's productivity and quality department (formerly the industrial engineering department) has fashioned a framework for BPR that also encompasses the company's continuous improvement and employee involvement efforts. Dubbed the Time-Based Continuous Improvement Approach (TBCIA), the program incorporates reengineering and employee involvement with more traditional industrial engineering (IE) tools and techniques to create an umbrella for "self-sufficient quality," or the transfer of change-related improvement skills to plant employees.

The nation's second largest manufacturer of incandescent, fluorescent and high-intensity discharge lighting products, OSRAM Sylvania employs 12,500 people in 25 manufacturing facilities in the United States, Canada, Puerto Rico and Mexico and its headquarters in Danvers, Mass. The word "OSRAM" appearing before the familiar Sylvania name refers to the Munich-based company, OSRAM GmbH (a subsidiary of Siemens A.G.), that purchased Sylvania's lighting products group from GTE Corp. in January 1993.

Reinventing the wheel
Led by Kevin Watts, director of productivity and quality, OSRAM Sylvania's IE group developed TBCIA as an alternative to the company's traditional approach of improving in bits and pieces. Watts and his team felt that the incremental method was not optimizing the organization, that patching leaks in the tire was not always enough to get the company where it needed to go. Reinventing the wheel was often what the road required. "TBCIA enables us to deliver [IE] tools and techniques to our plants under one banner, so that the matching of solutions to problems isn't disjointed or dysfunctional," Watts says. "Also, the reengineering aspect of it allows us to address challenges in a more visionary manner.

"Before," Watts continues, "product line managers, engineering managers, etc. would call to say, 'I need a setup reduction; I need a layout analysis.' Then many times, we would go to the facility and find out that they didn't really need what they asked for but a different tool altogether. Instead of a setup reduction, they might need an organizational analysis. Maybe the original problems were merely symptoms."

Now, under the aegis of TBCIA, the IE team goes into a facility to "tackle an entire business cycle that goes on under that plant's roof

— typically, from order entry to shipment," explains Steve Soffron, lead industrial engineer. "In a small company, you might analyze a longer cycle — for example, taking a look at more of the front end with sales and product development. At this company, those things are done centrally. So when we go into one of our plants, we start by asking, 'Just what do these people do, here?' Traditionally, the industrial engineer would only look at manufacturing. But we examine materials, purchasing and distribution as well."

The TBCIA seed was sown as long as three years ago, when Watts encouraged members of the IE team to attend conferences and industry seminars to soak up new developments in the field. Meetings on time compression and reengineering seemed particularly relevant to the company's current needs and, along with Watts's desire for an all-encompassing IE approach, helped spawn the TBCIA concept. In the fall of 1991, the IEs began to prepare for the first pilot project.

The first proposed pilot site was at a plant in Quebec, Canada. The managers there agreed to participate in a TBCIA project involving its high-intensity discharge (HID) line. But before the actual work was to begin, OSRAM purchased Sylvania and made decisions aimed at cutting costs. Unlike its U.S. plants, which each produce a single product line, the Canadian production site manufactures multiple product lines. After comparing the efficiencies of the Canadian HID production with those of other facilities, management decided to move the operation to the company's low-cost HID producer in New Hampshire. If time had been on the IE group's side, Watts says, things might have been different. "If we could have gotten into Canada sooner and started [TBCIA] — gone over their HID line, analyzed it and made improvements — who knows..."

As it turned out, a Pennsylvania plant underwent the first actual TBCIA pilot (see figure 1). Since then, TBCIA projects have been conducted at plants in New Hampshire, Kentucky and Mexico.

After the team put TBCIA together and performed the requisite number of "what ifs", they then cast feelers out to locations the team felt were progressive, were ready to jettison old formulas and try novel approaches. "We were very upfront with them," Soffron says. "Basically, we said: 'We have something new; we've gone over all the angles, checked under all the rocks, covered all the bases, but we don't have a track record yet. We're looking for a place to get started, and we'd like to work with you.' And, fortunately, some of the people responded, 'It sounds good to me, let's give it a shot.'"

TBCIA simply yields "the biggest bang for the buck," according to Watts, optimizing the tools the IE has at his or her disposal and making the most of the teamwork between the IEs and a plant's staff. Six of the 10-member IE staff work on TBCIA projects, serving first as surveyors, next as teachers and then as advisors. They perform the initial assessment, analyzing the results with plant personnel. Then the team imparts the necessary tools and techniques to the plant workers so they can employ these methods themselves, with guidance. Via these roles, the IEs hope to create long-term partnerships with the plants. This way, they no longer function just as a "pair of hands" to do the work of reengineering; IEs lead the way but foster a change-minded, self-reliant attitude among the plant staff.

Though obviously beneficial, "this approach is an engrossing, time-consuming way to go into a facility," Soffron says. "You need to provide for a fair amount of follow-up. After the first couple of months, you need to cycle back maybe three or four days a week."

"It's quite a change in management style," Watts adds. "This is new, and it isn't the only way we do business." Sometimes an assembly line problem needs just a tweak; reinventing the process isn't necessary. Also, Watts says, often a plant may call for just a single one-time tool, such as activity-based costing, and truly need just that. "But if you check back in couple of years, I think the percentage of pervasive, TBCIA-type projects will be much higher."

Emphasizing outcomes, not tasks
Concentrating on representative, big-volume products with apparent problems or opportunities, the team begins a TBCIA intervention by giving the plant manager an hour-long overview of the approach. "Then, if he responds positively — if he even sees half the potential benefit—we're asked to come back to talk with some of the plant staff, to whom we provide a similar overview," Watts explains. "If they, too, express some enthusiasm for a partnership, we next do an assessment. After examining one area of the plant's business, we discuss the results of our process mapping and other measurements. Then we get together with the plant staff to brainstorm potential solutions."

Envisioned as a continual cycle of reinvention and improvement, TBCIA consists of six steps: researching and mapping the business process; analyzing the results; identifying problems and prioritizing solutions; developing and implementing a BPR plan through employee involvement; measuring the results of the newly reengineered process; and standardizing the new, improved process.

To elicit employee input in the initial research phase, the

team conducts interviews, asking, basically, "If this were your candy store, how would you run it?" In the course of this questioning, the team uncovers barriers, the things that get in the way of a person doing an effective job (e.g., outdated equipment, political difficulties, ringing telephones). "Once we get some exposure to these barriers," Soffron says, "a lot of them can be done away with by someone else in the department or somebody one notch up in the organization. Usually, when people can say, 'Do you realize what sort of burden I'm dealing with day after day?' and know they can be open and voice their concerns, the barriers begin to disappear."

The information gleaned from interviews forms the foundation for composing a process map, or breaking down the whole business cycle into steps. Typically, a business cycle within a plant extends from order entry to scheduling, procurement, receiving, storage, production, inspection, warehousing and, finally, distribution. These steps are matched to the person who "owns" or is responsible for that step. How much each step costs in time and money also is determined.

Next in the TBCIA cycle, the IEs analyze the results of the process map to determine which of the steps are "value-added," or essential to the desires of the customer. The idea being that reengineering emphasizes ultimate outcomes rather than initial tasks, with the desires of the customer paramount. "In our experience," Soffron says, "the great majority of a process's steps — maybe even 80 percent of them — do not add value in the customer's eyes. If you were to ask a customer, 'If we were to do this in the making of the product, would you be willing to pay for that step that costs $1.25 as a part of the [product's] price?' Most often, the answer would be: 'No.' " As part of the mapping, the "nonvalue-added" steps are marked for elimination, if possible. Not all such steps can be abandoned, though, because certain nonvalue-added steps are necessary to progress to other steps that the customer does value.

Following the analysis of value-added versus nonvalue-added, teams are formed, comprising those employees who actually do the work in question and who possess some degree of autonomy. The team devises a plan for reengineering the process to maximize the value-added steps and minimize the nonvalue-added ones, using the IE tools and techniques deemed appropriate — including those both technical (e.g., implementation of quick changeover, level loading, continuous-flow production, just-in-time manufacturing, ergonomics, vendor partnerships) and social (self-managed work teams, team

The following charts depict the opportunity for improvement in two TBCIA pilot applications. Each chart serves as a "before picture," reflecting the value-added steps and time involved in the manufacture of a lighting product. In reengineering a business process, the aim is to eliminate as many nonvalue-added steps in the process as possible, thereby increasing the percentage of steps inherently valuable to the customer.

Product One

Process	Total Number of Steps	Number of Value-Added Steps	Value-Added Time in Hours	Total Process Time in Days
Forecasting/Planning/Scheduling	25	5	17	2
Procurement	41	8	7.75	10
Supply Parts	10	3	Unknown	43
Receiving	37	2	1.25	48
Coil Waxing	23	6	24.5	3
Shipping/Receiving	39	2	.5	28
Capsule Making	55	14	64.5	15
Lamp Assembly	55	14	116	11
Finished Goods Processing	49	4	.75	4
Total	334	58	232.25	164
Value-Added Percentage		17.37	5.9	

Product Two

Process	Total Number of Steps	Number of Value-Added Steps	Value-Added Time in Hours	Total Process Time in Days
Planning/Scheduling/Procurement	52	8	12	16
Supply Parts	10	3	Unknown	53
Receiving	36	2	1.25	2
Mount Production	61	15	17	5
Shipping/Receiving	39	2	.5	4
Capsule Making	52	13	71.25	12
Transfer	47	3	.75	5
Lamp Finishing	34	15	14	3
Finished Goods Processing	68	2	.5	8
Quality Review	46	7	.75	5
Total	445	70	118	113
Value-Added Percentage		15.73	4.35	

Figure 1. Charting Value with the Time-Based Continuous Improvement Approach

problem solving, work redesign, interpersonal skills training, organizational restructure, multiskill cross training, skill-based compensation).

After the team reengineers the process, it gauges the results of the new operation. Watts insists that measurement is fundamental to any successful BPR project, with determining base lines and discerning first-pass yield (the percentage of products or services acceptably completed on the first attempt without rework) serving as prime yardsticks along with pinpointing barriers and identifying value-added versus nonvalue-added activities. Once satisfactory, the newly reengineered process is standardized, using a program for continuous improvement that takes advantage of systems such as ISO 9000's regimen of quality surveys and internal audits as well as relies on a culture of sustained employee involvement.

"Situations like the time-card example make people aware that they should be questioning whether barriers exist or what is value-added time and what isn't," Watts says. "That payroll clerk had no concept of [suggesting change] as part of her job. She thought her job was to take a couple of hours a week filling in social security numbers. The point [of TBCIA] is for us to be aware of why we're all here. We're here to satisfy the customer. People don't always think that way, though. They just come to their jobs and do their thing and aren't always alert or open to evaluating what they do according to its value or nonvalue for the customer. But once they're awakened to this approach, they love it. It enriches their jobs, whether they're hourly workers or managers."

Barriers and bandaids
The TBCIA teams have surmounted most of the barriers they have encountered so far by engendering communication and forward thinking. For instance: Materials are trucked from a plant in Mexico to a facility in Kentucky, with the vehicles filled with 75 percent finished goods, 20 percent subassemblies and five percent waste. In this example, the Kentucky plant's import/export receiver was industrious, squaring away the larger amount of finished goods first, as was standard operating procedure. But production was waiting on the subassemblies; four or five hours would go by while line crews sat idle. A volatile situation between the production and receiving departments began to simmer, with production grousing "We're waiting!" and receiving countering "We're working on it!" The IEs formed a team with members of each department, and over a couple of weeks

and several meetings, the team decided that it was less expensive in terms of dormant manpower and subsequent overtime to get the subassemblies to production first. By processing the subassemblies as soon as possible, the receiving department cut production's waiting period from the four or five hours to one hour. Also, not insignificantly, the new rationale was explained tactfully to the finished goods people.

The benefits of the solution were dual: Tactically, the plant gained production time efficiencies and reduced costly overtime. Strategically, "I think there was just as much value culturally, getting people to work together toward a common goal," says Judith Paul, lead industrial engineer on the Kentucky project. "Separate departments can have a tendency to concentrate too much on their individual goals without considering how these goals relate to the company's overall objectives."

A second anecdote comes from Paul's Kentucky experience. In its manufacture of lighting capsules, the Kentucky plant receives mounts from Mexico. The Kentucky operation's production manager would order 1,000 mounts from the warehouse, but consistently 1,296 would arrive. For a while, he tried to send the extra back, but the hassles of handling and counting the small mounts forced him to produce the 296 additional capsules instead. These extra capsules cost an average of two days a month in overproduction and sat on the floor as space-consuming excess inventory. Cross-functional teams from Kentucky and Mexico discovered that this particular stock was packed in six boxes of 216 mounts and stored in a larger tote. Warehouse workers in Kentucky were simply grabbing a whole tote to cover the order, rounding up and over the amount rather than pulling and separating the exact number requested. By having the facility in Mexico identify the type and quantity of the small inner boxes, the Kentucky plant could change the way it pulled and processed orders — thereby shaving one and one-half days a month off the overproduction time.

The capsule production line continues to receive some extra stock, which it still produces, but the amount ordered and the number received are much closer now. Through continuous improvement, even these numbers should decrease. In this instance, the Kentucky plant gained the tactical benefits of fewer overtime hours, reduced inventory and more warehouse space. And, strategically, it was a prime example of cooperation between not only two different departments but two different facilities.

As problems occur and months and years pass, barriers can take the form of quick-fix bandaids that have been applied as a way of meeting short-term expectations like inspections, quotas and deadlines. "These bandaids often end up staying on indefinitely," Watts says. "And whole systems grow around these flawed quick fixes, so that what was designed to be a temporary solution can grow to be a long-term hindrance."

Many times, elaborate procedures develop around decisions that were fine once upon a time but have since become outmoded, arbitrary and counterproductive. For example, at the Pennsylvania facility, electrical connections for cathode-ray tubes are handled in 40,000-piece lots, a quantity that has turned into a pain to handle. In the 1960s, the production lines ran 40,000 pieces a day, with these lots filling a day's work. With production speeds having long since increased, the facility's daily run now totals from 100,000 to 120,000 pieces. So, what was once efficient is now a case of: "That's the way we've always done it." Affecting everything from material handling equipment to paperwork, the 40,000-piece lot is not necessarily divisible for modern bins, racks or machinery. For the line to run more efficiently, fewer bigger lots could be necessary or possibly more smaller lots. But, Watts points out, entrenched notions of "But it fits in this gray tote here, see?" prevail. "The question," he says, "should be one of: 'Why don't we just order a different-sized tote to match the optimum lot for the current equipment?'" Even though this seems like a straightforward solution to a simple problem, the dilemma has been recognized but is yet unresolved.

Another of the consistent inconsistencies the IEs encounter as they interview plant employees is that the actual time it takes to do things is always much longer than people think. An example you've probably heard before relates how an insurance adjuster says it only takes him one hour to process a claim. So how come it really takes the company two weeks to process the claim? Because it sits in the adjuster's in-basket for one week, four days and seven hours before he gets a chance to start work on it. Though rarely counted, in the real world that time counts. A real-world example: At the Kentucky facility, IEs told the purchasing manager that they had determined it took two days to process purchase orders; incredulous, he said, 'No way. It takes one day, I know.' Even though confronted by the facts, he still had a hard time setting aside his closely held assumptions. The facts were that he was waiting until late in the day to sign the purchase orders, so they were missing the day's mail pickup. Consequently, they were not truly processed until the next day, in effect, tacking on an entire extra day to the process. Once he was convinced of this, the purchasing manager immediately altered his schedule in order to sign the purchase orders early in the afternoon so they could make that day's mail, thus pruning the extra day.

Watts points out that administrative processes such as purchasing are often neglected while trying to squeeze as much value out of the value-added steps on the production floor as possible. "So much attention has been placed on production — improving and honing, reducing and enhancing —that the company often forgets about all the overhead expense, administrative waste, lead time, excess inventory and processing costs that happen in front of and behind production," he says.

"Business process reengineering broadens the scope of the IE," Watts continues. "Before, if we went to purchasing and asked what was their first-pass yield, they'd say 'Huh, what are you talking about? I don't make light bulbs. Why are you asking me that? My first-pass yield is 100 percent. I get all my purchase orders out.' People don't realize that measurements like first-pass yield apply to more than just manufacturing. If purchasing gets a number wrong and asks a supplier for 10,000 instead of 100,000, we're not going to make the schedule that month."

Practicing what you preach
In helping others help themselves through TBCIA, the group has had its own obstacles to overcome. Finding an efficient means of mapping processes was an initial challenge; the IEs experimented for months with a variety of ways of getting business processes on paper graphically — first, they tested AutoCad; then they tried creating the maps by hand. When neither method met their demands, they sought advice from well-known consulting firms in the field that rely on process maps as an integral part of their approaches. From these suggestions, they chose EasyFlow for personal computers and have been using it since.

Considerably more daunting than software shopping have been two other obstacles: mastering the lengthy interviewing process and addressing fears about job security.

Exposing the root cause of a business process impasse requires information, data culled through digging and questioning. The TBCIA teams conducted hours upon hours of interviews in their first projects. These protracted sessions were arduous, taking up managers' and line crews' precious time. The meetings also led to interminable days of transcribing tapes, typing notes and reviewing them for accuracy. It became evident that the separation of wheat from chaff was taking much too long.

"We could see that we were wasting people's time with a cumbersome interview process," Soffron says. "So we trimmed it down, holding orientation meetings not one-on-one as we did them originally but with the whole team at once. We also refocused the interviews down a layer in the organization, talking with the line people right away. We even began to map out the processes right in the interviews. This sped everything up enormously."

By speaking first with those employees who know the intricacies of time, tools and technique first hand, the IEs are able to walk their talk about time compression and efficiency. "We try to use [TBCIA] principles on our own processes," Soffron says. "So if we're examining the receiving of raw materials, we don't want to speak to the materials manager, we want to talk to the receiver — the guy who unloads the truck, puts the stuff away and does the paperwork. He's the only guy who can step us through all the various steps of the process. This way, we're considering end results first, not just going through all the motions... We're trying to practice what we preach."

Unlike the newly streamlined interview process, concerns over job security present a recurring hurdle. Many times when faced with reengineering, employees are scared that the reinvention of their functions or those around them means the company will cut people left and right. These fears can impede reengineering, from the interview phase to final implementation. "[TBCIA] can become a sensitive issue," Soffron says. "Because people think, 'Geez, if they really knew what I was doing... I'm afraid to expose myself.' Those are real fears that we'll probably always have to deal with. Our response is 'Let's talk substitution rather than elimination.' "

To date, new efficiencies created by TBCIA have not resulted in any layoffs of permanent employees, although in one case some temporary workers were no longer needed after the streamlining of inspection procedures. As a means of allaying anxieties over an impending TBCIA project, Watts asks plant managers to address the job-security issue before the team arrives. According to Watts, the plant manager should make the point that the danger is not as real as people presume, because companies that eliminate nonvalue-added activities will satisfy more customers — thereby gaining a competitive edge and with it new customers. "Successful companies are those that become more customer responsive, getting the product out the door in 20 days instead of 100," Soffron says. "By getting yourself in this position, you're going to get more business. So not only do you not have to lay people off, you might even be able to expand."

Fulfilling needs

Fundamental to the success of TBCIA are not only the industrial engineering skills of the IEs but their talents as salesmen. For TBCIA to be implemented at one plant or for it to grow into a way of doing business companywide, the IEs must sell the approach's benefits to three separate constituencies, each with different needs.

Selling TBCIA to corporate executives, plant management and facility personnel requires Watts and his team to answer the universal question: "What is TBCIA going to do for me?" What may enrapture an executive vice president may not thrill a plant manager, and what may excite a line worker may put a chairman to sleep.

For TBCIA to address the concerns of plant staff, it must not threaten job security. But the approach also needs to: minimize an employee's daily on-the-job frustrations and attendant stress; enable the employee to respond faster to his customer, whether internal or external; identify and reduce the cultural, technical and procedural barriers that hinder the employee from doing a quality job; and allow the employee to question his habitual activities and act on low-risk changes. Again, the benefits of reengineering are relative. A project may free up 15 percent more floor space, which is a great motivator for a plant manager. But what motivates a line worker is something else entirely; the project motivates him because it reduces the number of steps in the material handling process, making his job easier.

Plant managers want to hear that TBCIA: reduces lead time, lowers scrap, frees up space and time, simplifies complicated tasks, eliminates unnecessary work and improves communication among internal and external suppliers and customers. Though even when presented with his operation's room for improvement in black and white, a plant manager may exhibit denial. According to Watts, "When you go to a plant manager—who runs a $100 million business — and tell him that you're there to help him reduce barriers, most often he looks at you funny and says, 'What barriers? What do you mean it takes me 150 days to get a shipment out the door? Bull. I know I can get one out in a month.' Well, we tell him that he probably can get *one* out in a month. But we're calculating how long it takes to process the average shipment.

"Those who have been searching for a solution tend to welcome the facts with enthusiasm," Watts continues. "Those who are confronted by facts that they never asked for often deny it at first. But the denial eventually begins to melt away. It has to. You can't argue with the numbers."

To thaw the skepticism of executive management, the productivity and quality department must convince it that TBCIA will generate improved quality, reduced costs, enhanced customer responsiveness, lower inventories, increased reliability and heightened innovation. So far, the IEs have been able to secure a circumscribed measure of support. But Soffron and the rest of the team realize that this is all they can expect and are confident that this is all they should need. "In any organization, support isn't given; support is earned," Soffron says. "What we got [from OSRAM] was a vote of confidence. The way we'll get true support is through our success. After we've had the chance to work at a location for three or four years and can say 'Look at what we've accomplished,' then we'll get real support. Management will say, 'Wow, let's do more of this; let's gear up.' "

The IEs have taken a step-by-step strategy for advancing TBCIA. Understanding that change in an organization as large as OSRAM Sylvania often comes from the middle rather than the top, the IEs want to steadily build a base of support among plant managers. Only then will TBCIA develop staying power, not by pushing it as an executive decision. "With many organizations, you have this corporate program-of-the-month-type thing," Soffron says. "You know, you get the T-shirts and the banners, and people think, 'I wonder how long this one's going to last?' Those things just don't fly, they just kind of fade away. Having seen this, we don't want to do [TBCIA] that way. We want to bring about a lasting cultural change, a new way of doing things.

"Instead of having a president or vice president shove it down people's throats, which never works," Soffron continues, "we hope these individual programs are successful enough that word gets around and more and more plants call us up to say, 'You know what you did for the Pennsylvania plant? We'd like you to come work with us on that.' In the long run, our chances of making TBCIA a permanent, company-wide approach are much better by establishing a gradual track record of successes with those plants who are open to it than by announcing: 'All locations will commence TBCIA effective January 1.'"

New means for better ends

The members of the productivity and quality department know that if companies keep doing things the way they have always done them, they won't be doing them for much longer. Busting paradigms can reap crucial tactical rewards. The forecasts for TBCIA's eventual benefits are substantial: 30 percent to 70 percent lead-time reduction, 5 percent to 25 percent productivity increase, 15 percent to 40 percent scrap/rework decrease, 6 percent to 45 percent materials-cost reduction, 5 percent to 60 percent inventory reduction, 60 percent to 90 percent setup reduction, 10 percent to 35 percent space savings. But notwithstanding that impressive list, the IEs realize that reengineering creates new means for better ends, generating more holistic benefits than simple cost reduction or improved labor efficiency. Enhanced employee commitment, increased internal communication and improved customer service are projected as immediate strategic benefits of TBCIA.

"Reengineering forces you to look at the big picture," Soffron says. "To be a world-class competitor, we need to think that way in order to satisfy our customers faster and with higher quality than the competition. We see it, really, as the only way to survive in the global economy of the future."

A
Case Study
by
Susan Taylor

Patent And Trademark Office

In spite of Vice President Al Gore's initiative, few federal government agencies have actively embraced the concept of business process reengineering (BPR). One notable exception is the Patent and Trademark Office (PTO) of the Department of Commerce. Already one of the best managed agencies in the federal government, the PTO is revamping the application process for both patents and trademarks and expects to save tens of millions of dollars every year once the redesigned systems are fully implemented.

The new processes will take full advantage of electronic technology to achieve huge reductions in labor and printing costs, as well as allow innovative and flexible management techniques such as work-at-home programs. Responsibility and authority will be concentrated in fewer employees through job enrichment and restructuring, and the level of service provided to PTO's customers will improve. The redesigned trademark application process also will meet upcoming international trademark requirements.

Technology catches up with needs
PTO is responsible for issuing and maintaining permanent records on all U.S. patents and trademarks. The patent side has a staff of about 4,000, and issues about 2,000 new patents each week. At present, all applications are in paper form and are enclosed in "file wrappers" or file jackets. PTO also is perhaps the largest repository of technical literature in the entire world. All documents and information related to patents dating back more than 200 years are stored in a space about the size of a football field.

The seeds for reengineering in PTO were planted almost ten years ago, when a plan was written for replacing the paper-based patent application process with an Electronic File Wrapper (EFW).

"About 300,000 patent applications are in process at any one time, and the related documents are trucked from building to building, moved around in handcarts, filed, unfiled, updated and refiled," explained L. Liddle, acting director of PTO's Business Reengineering Team (BRT). "They are lost, and they are found. The whole process is subject to errors, very labor intensive and time consuming."

The concept of electronic filing was excellent, but premature. Adequate technology simply was not in widespread use by applicants at the time, and PTO could not afford the time or money necessary to convert all of the paper documents into electronic text and graphic programs.

After almost ten years of explosive computer technology growth, the idea of electronic filing was reassessed. A cost-benefit analysis completed in December 1992 showed that EFW could save hundreds of millions in printing costs alone, along with thousands of staff years of work over a 10-year period.

Those figures quickly reached the attention of the Commissioner of Patents and Trademarks, the Office of Management and Budget (OMB), and Capitol Hill. PTO created a BPR organization, and preliminary reengineering plans were being formulated as early as March 1993.

At the same time, the trademark portion of the office was facing major changes in how its applications would be handled. The trademark side is much smaller, with a staff of about 350, including about 180 trademark examining attorneys. Reengineering within this group has its roots in two areas.

The first root cause results from the Madrid Protocols, which in effect create an international trademark application/registration. The enabling legislation for this set of international agreements is before Congress now and is expected to be passed soon. Trademark application requirements under the Madrid Protocols are significantly different from the current processes for U.S. trademark registrations. Rather than create a second process to accompany current U.S. procedures, PTO realized it would be best to engineer a whole new process that would embody the requirements of both U.S. and Madrid Protocol applications.

The second impetus for reengineering within the trademark

office was PTO's decision to establish a pilot work-at-home project. This project will allow trademark examining attorneys to spend several days a week doing their work from home, rather than spending that time in the office.

"That requires the development of new techniques for processing and implies the existence of electronic files," explained Liddle. "We also expect it to have a huge impact on management structure and management practices."

Reengineering projects for both patent and trademark applications processes are being done in parallel under the auspices of the new BPR organization. Of the two, the trademark application project is the more all-encompassing in that it includes a complete redesign of every aspect of the trademark process, including the way examining attorneys do their searches.

On the patent side, the EFW will have its main impact on support personnel who process papers pertaining to applications, although some effects will be felt by all patent examiners and employees who handle, inspect, examine, modify or make decisions based on the patent application and its contents. The EFW project offers greater potential savings simply due to the sheer number of applications involved.

Ideal climate for reengineering

The common perception of federal government agencies is not one that includes the ability to effect radical changes to achieve breakthrough improvements. Nevertheless, Liddle believes the BPR effort within the PTO has every opportunity for success.

"All the right things have been done so far," he pointed out. "It's almost an ideal climate for a reengineering effort. We have the full support of the Commissioner and Executive Staff. They have set up a reasonable reengineering structure and organization and divorced it from the Information Systems group, which is important.

"We also have been able to train close to 300 top level executives about what business reengineering is and what some of the tools are. And, of course, we have their implicit commitment because their bosses are committed," he added.

The key to successful reengineering is absolute commitment from the top. Bruce A. Lehman, Assistant Secretary of Commerce and Commissioner of Patents and Trademarks, is strongly supportive of the PTO reengineering effort, and views the project as critical not only to PTO, but to the Department of Commerce, as well.

"Secretary [of Commerce] Ron Brown is a strong supporter of the business process reengineering program because he is aware of — and is committed to — turning around the private sector's general impressions of government operations. The PTO's program, I think, will not only help strengthen U.S. intelligence property systems overall by improving the delivery of services, but also BPR will help serve as a powerful rebuttal to those in private industry who say government can't change, particularly because it's [the PTO BPR program] based on tried and true techniques used by America's best run corporations for making businesses more 'user-friendly,'" Lehman explained.

A political appointee, Lehman feels the BPR program fits quite well the Clinton Administration's objective for reinventing government. "The project easily made the transition to the Clinton administration, largely because it simply makes sense," said Liddle. "It is a Good Thing to do—capital G, Capital T. I don't think it will be subject to the political winds of change."

Closely following Michael Hammer's BPR model, PTO established a Business Council made up of executives at the highest level of the organization to act as the BPR steering committee. The council, which is ultimately responsible to Lehman, is made up of Assistant Commissioner for Patents (Designate) Lawrence Goffney, Assistant Commissioner for Trademarks (Designate) Phillip Hampton, Assistant Commissioner for Public Services and Administration Theresa A. Brelsford, Assistant Commissioner for Finance & Planning Bradford R. Huther, and Assistant Commissioner for External Affairs Michael Kirk.

The Business Council is responsible for establishing overall agency and BPR goals, setting priorities and allocating resources, approving final process designs and implementation strategies, conducting major project milestone reviews, and reviewing and approving the implemented redesigned processes. Issues that cannot be resolved by the Council are referred to the Commissioner for final resolution.

To provide technical support, the Council created the BRT in March 1993, and staffed it with the brightest, most capable people available. In addition to Liddle, who has a background in systems development, the team includes two patent examiners, one trademark examining attorney, and experts in finance and administrative processes, among others. (See figure 1 for a complete list of BRT core team members and their experience.)

L. Liddle, Acting Director — Former Acting Deputy Director for Systems Development and Maintenance. Led the development of on-line patent search systems.

Jo-Anne Barnard — Attorney who has spent much of her career with the General Services Administration. Most recently involved in the development of PTO space requirements for the next decade.

Bo Bounkong — Former patent examiner. Dual degrees in industrial engineering and operations research, and currently pursuing a degree in systems engineering.

Mary Frances Bruce — Former senior trademark attorney. Participated in development of functional requirements for automated trademark search system.

Bridgette Carson — Will graduate with a degree in Accounting in 1994.

John Serlemitsos — Engineer with background in OMB.

Bob Spar — More than 20 years experience as a senior patent examiner.

Mary Turowski — Former management analyst with broad knowledge of PTO processes.

Melissa Wood — Part-time team member. Senior at Howard University with plans to attend law school after graduation.

Ad Hoc member:

Frances Michalkewicz — Director of PTO's Office of Long Range Planning and Evaluation.

Figure 1. Business Reengineering Team Core Staff

The BRT, along with about 30 top level executives and representatives from each of the three employee bargaining units within PTO, attended a reengineering course put on by the Defense Department. This course introduced the team to the basic concepts, tools and methodologies used in reengineering. In addition, individual BRT members have attended a variety of other BPR courses, including a symposium on reengineering in federal government done at Harvard and a series of seminars put on by Computer Science Corp. (CSC) Quantum, a consulting group whose customers are almost 100 percent private industry.

The BRT is charged with the responsibility to develop and maintain comprehensive project plans, provide BPR training, facilitate the analysis of current business processes and the development of new processes, develop strategies for soliciting external and internal customer inputs, help design appropriate automated systems, develop transition plans, and coordinate all activities integral to achieving objectives.

Liddle emphasized that his team is not responsible for creating the new processes, but instead will advise and assist project teams from the two units to develop their own new processes. These project teams will be supported by the Assistant Commissioners for Trademarks and Patents, who will act as Program Sponsors within their units. These BPR champions serve as liaisons with the rest of top management and play a key role as project monitors, critics and advisors.

Two full-time project managers will coordinate and control the reengineering projects on a day-to-day basis. The project manager for the trademark side is Sharon Marsh, a senior trademark examining attorney. A senior patent examining official will be selected soon to manage the patent office EFW project. These individuals will assign specific project tasks to team members, monitor project status, and manage communications through council briefings, PTO-wide briefings and external briefings.

Under the leadership of the project manager, various reengineering project teams will focus on the whole spectrum of areas to be addressed. Individual project teams have been formed for project management, as-is modeling, to-be modeling, benchmarking, financial analysis, human resources, facility planning, systems development, process measurement, strategic planning, customer relations, health and safety, security, systems requirements, systems testing, procurement, policy and procedures, public services and organizational development.

Five-year plan for parallel projects

At nine members, the BRT is too small to accomplish alone all the tasks necessary to design and implement the massive projects underway. Management Technology Associates (MTA), a consulting firm headquartered in Huntsville, Ala., and its principal sub-contractor Price Waterhouse provide an additional 20 staff years of people per year. MTA has provided significant training support for the BRT, as well as for the executive staff and senior level managers. The firm also is designing the training program for employees whose jobs will be affected by BPR.

PTO is using a just-in-time cascade approach to training. Senior managers in a given area are trained first, after which they begin high level BPR tasks. Continuing in a cascade effect, other managers, supervisors, and employees at lower and lower levels are trained just before they are needed to flesh out their level of detail.

Together with MTA, the BRT has developed a five-year plan to complete the two reengineering projects in parallel. The BPR program is divided into seven phases: Enterprise Strategy; Business Reengineering Strategy; As-Is Modeling; To-Be Modeling; Transition Planning; Implementation; and Evaluation and Continuous Improvement.

In the first phase, the Business Council identified PTO's mission, values, vision, goals, objectives and critical success factors. The second phase was similar, but tailored to the specific reengineering task. That phase is being completed concurrently with subsequent phases and is expected to be complete by mid-1994.

During the third phase, current business practices were measured and documented. Senior managers, in a classic top down approach, were asked to develop detailed models of the current processes. "We wanted to make sure we understood enough about the way things are done now to effectively develop a view of the way things ought to be," explained Liddle.

Phase three was completed by the end of February 1994, and the to-be design team immediately began developing target visions for the two projects. Both current and target process models were developed using IDEF (integration definitions) modeling techniques. IDEF uses graphics and text modeling to depict critical activities, processes, and information used in day-to-day business processes. Activity-based cost analysis techniques were then mapped to the IDEF process models.

Transition planning will begin in the last quarter of 1994, and implementation is expected to get underway in early 1995. Full implementation is expected by 1999.

Taking a fresh view of the process
The council and BRT were very careful in selecting to-be design team members. "As we do the target process, we want people who are innovative, imaginative and not restrained by 200 years of history," Liddle explained.

"The PTO really is very efficient already, given the limitations of what you can do with paper," he continued. "The processes are well rooted in history and in need. They have been analyzed again and again. So it presents a real challenge to make dramatic improvements. Short of the introduction of automated tools and techniques, I doubt very much if we could significantly improve the processes."

However, he was careful to point out that PTO will not just automate the manual system. "We are designing a new process that will take full advantage of automated tools and techniques, but we are doing that with as fresh a view and vision as we can," he said. "I hope we will not be fettered by any precedence or 200 years of institutional memory."

As the target vision is developed, the BRT will build cost models for it, which will then be compared to base line costs, so that true costs versus benefits can be identified, including the ultimate impact on personnel.

The target visioning process is expected to take about seven months. During this phase, the Business Council must make several fundamental decisions very early in the process. For example, should enriched jobs be developed where one person, assisted by information technology, could do work performed by four or five people today, or should the office continue to have simple jobs done by less empowered clerks or personnel. The ultimate choice probably will fall somewhere in the range between these two extremes.

Another major decision to be faced soon involves the implementation sequence for EFW. Work in the patent office is done in three major stages. Pre-examination processing includes administrative type activities that prepare the application before an examiner sees it. The second stage is the examination process, during which the examiner works with the applicant to amend or modify the application to bring it into a patentable condition. At the end of that process, the examiner determines whether it is patentable or not. If it is, then the application goes into post-examination, which includes processes that result in the printing of the patent and the publication of various materials associated with it. Publication is done in many media, including paper, microfilm, magnetic tape and CD ROM.

One implementation sequence would be according to the process sequence itself: pre-exam process first, then exam, then post-exam. Using that sequence, a wave of electronic applications would go through the process, and each time they reach the next stage, ideally the system would have been extended to support EFW.

Liddle pointed out, however, that one of the biggest areas of savings is in the printing preparation process. "If the priority is in saving money as quickly as possible, we would be better off building the tail end of the system first," he said. "We could then simply ask the applicant to send an electronic version of the patent only after the examiner has determined the application is patentable."

Complexity of the pieces involved also is a major factor in determining the implementation sequence. "It would be nice to develop the simplest pieces first, so you can start to get a better understanding of how it really is being implemented, and then fine tune the more complex pieces at a more leisurely pace," Liddle explained.

Other critical decisions the council must make during this phase involve strategies for labor/management relations, training and facilities planning.

Setting goals for a moving target

All during the target vision phase, the Business Council is continuing to develop the strategic direction called for in Phase II. From this work will come the fully-defined BPR mission, goals, objectives, critical success factors and measures of performance that can be applied at all levels of the target process. Strategic planning and goal setting is being done by the director of long-range planning and eight senior officials, including the budget officer, personnel officer, executive assistant to the Commissioner, patent examining group directors, and Liddle.

For benchmarks, the group is looking at private industry as well as other federal government agencies. In the area of electronic filing, the group will look to the Securities and Exchange Commission's EDGAR project and the National Academy of Science's process for grant applications. For publishing processes, they may try to benchmark with Publishers' Clearing House or the Chemical Abstract Society. The group also wants to find a world class mailroom operation for benchmarking. Liddle also believes the PTO could learn from major corporations in the private sector such as Texas Instruments, Boeing and IBM.

Liddle pointed out that potential changes in legislation also may have a major effect on goals. "We have to be ready to respond to those changes as necessary. They will impose new goals and may cause us to jettison what have been fondly held goals for the past couple of decades because they no longer apply."

For example, under current legislation, a patent applicant is protected from the date the application is filed, but the term of the patent expires 17 years from the date the patent actually is issued. Thus, a long turnaround time between application and patent determination may actually benefit the applicant.

One likely change in legislation would create a 20-year term, under which the patent would be good 20 years from the date of filing, regardless of when the actual patent is issued. Under that scenario, the applicant would want the patent issued as quickly as possible to maximize profits from license fees.

Using current processes, it takes an average of 18 months after filing to issue a patent. EFW should cut that time dramatically, although exact goals are not yet established. "We will have to talk to inventors about what they think goals should be, and then temper that with reality and what is technologically possible," Liddle explained.

Customer input is critical
In addition to patent timing goals, PTO believes customer input on their whole range of needs and requirements will be critical to developing a usable system. The BPR projects currently underway target only trademark and patent applicants as customers. Eventually, the council wants to extend the project to include end users of the technical literature associated with patents.

The customer survey needs of BPR dovetail nicely with one of the Presidential directives that are part of the National Performance Review underway in the Clinton Administration. An executive order established last September requires agencies that serve the public to define who their customers are, and to develop and post service standards equal to the best in the business. Under the directive, agencies must benchmark standards, survey their customers and provide them with alternative choices and means for redress. Although the goals for this directive are not exactly the same as the BPR project, a great deal of overlap is expected.

Final plans are not yet in place as to which customers to talk to for BRT purposes versus those for other customer service initiatives. "This whole customer identification business is no easier in the federal government than it is for anybody else," Liddle said.

The BRT has identified those customers who will be alpha and beta test sites for the new application processes, but a full-blown survey of a truly representative sample of customers may take a bit longer. Under the Paperwork Reduction Act, the OMB must approve any solicited customer surveys that involve more than nine customers. While awaiting this approval, PTO has sought preliminary customer input by announcing its interest and asking for volunteers. Survey volunteers are not subject to OMB approval.

As it turns out, the volunteers who responded represent a broad spectrum of customer types, from major patent filing companies, to major law firms that represent companies, all the way down to the individual inventor who acts as his own patent attorney. Starting in late February 1994, these volunteers were put into focus groups and asked about how they create patent applications and how they handle correspondence with PTO, among other issues.

Liddle also wants specific input from PTO's "best" customers. "I want to talk to our 50 biggest customers, in terms of number of applications submitted, because we will serve them and us best if we manage to mesh our processes," he explained. These customers include major corporations such as IBM, Eastman Kodak and General Electric, among others.

Customer input will be especially important as the PTO begins developing the software that will be used for submitting applications. "We have to develop software that will work with the applicants' existing word processing software, and there is a fairly significant risk associated with that," Liddle said. "We will have to keep our software in sync with a multiplicity of word processing software produced by Microsoft or Wordperfect or whomever."

Long term, PTO expects patent application software to be developed by the commercial sector to meet PTO specifications. For the short term, however, the Business Council has determined that developing custom software is the most expedient solution.

While they are not inconsequential, the information system portions of PTO's reengineering projects do not rely on emerging technologies and, in general, are not expected to be overwhelmingly difficult.

Making the transition is the acid test

Liddle believes the most difficult aspect of reengineering in PTO will be making the transition from current processes to the target processes. The two BPR projects are so pervasive, they will ultimately involve almost every organization within the agency.

"This is the hardest part and the longest part," he commented. "When you look at how far this ripples through the organization, it just doesn't stop. You can't pick out one thing that is more important than another, because they all have to be done for the implementation to proceed smoothly."

The BRT has put together a consolidated transition schedule that already includes some 350 activities that range from space planning to health and safety, from security to labor/management relations and training, and many, many others. For example, finding space for the new processes in PTO is not straightforward. The agency is allocated space by the General Services Administration, and space planning must be done years in advance to ensure that funding is there.

"We also have to worry about health and safety considerations such as concerns over toner dust from printers or radiation from CRTs. We may have to relamp entire buildings to put in more appropriate lighting," Liddle added.

Security will be an issue on two levels. On one level, the office maintains the contents of patent applications in confidence until the patents are issued. (This is not true for trademark applications.) However, since the agency provides public services on a dial-up basis, the new system must incorporate automated system security to adequately protect sensitive data.

Physical security also must be addressed. "We're going to have thousands of terminals about the office," explained Liddle. "The public comes and goes at will, as they should be able to do. How do we make sure an unauthorized person cannot walk up to a workstation that happens to be vacant and start browsing through our confidential databases?"

Even the motor pool will be affected. Since data archiving probably will be done with a communications link to a storage facility in Pennsylvania, trucks will no longer be transporting paper files back and forth to warehouses.

Certainly labor/management relations will represent one of the biggest transition issues to be addressed in the coming months. "I think the prospect of reengineering is terrifying to bargaining units, just as it is terrifying to managers," said Liddle. "We're going to see a flattening of the organization, and lots and lots of people are going to be affected. We must develop a rational labor/management relations strategy for addressing issues that naturally arise out of the implementation of any reengineering process. To a certain extent those arrangements have to conform to whatever agreements we have in place with the unions, as well as any kind of initiatives that are taken to build different arrangements for working with the unions. There is a partnership council of PTO managers and union officials that hopefully will provide a forum for beginning to address those issues.

"We also have to set up a routine means of communicating to all our employees," he continued. "What we're doing, how we're doing it, how it's shaping up, but with a sense of perspective so that they can understand what is certain and what is speculative. We have to try to allay their concerns and address their concerns at the same time. To be honest, we can't make this work without employees. No one in the agency wants to see a disaffected workforce. We're going to have to take some heroic measures to address the concerns and needs of our employees."

Job retraining will be another huge undertaking. The knowledge, skills and abilities required of the EFW employees probably will be much different from those held by the current workforce.

"Most of our workforce is not particularly computer literate, so we have to make them computer literate," said Liddle. "That will require the development of a very, very aggressive training program. We have to rewrite thousands of position descriptions, establish new measures of performance for hundreds of employees, develop strategies for how we will coordinate the implementation with our employee bargaining units, and so on."

PTO also has begun gradually contracting out certain low-skilled functions in anticipation of reengineering. "We'll have a much better sense in about six months of what the precise staff reductions will be. I can see that we probably will have to develop a very aggressive outplacement program, possibly based on a model set up by the Department of Defense," he added.

Long-term commitment is necessary

In spite of a few start-up pains, Liddle is pleased with PTO's reengineering project, so far. He attributes the early success to the excellent climate and support his team has received from the top levels of management. However, he believes the hardest work is still ahead, and the possibility of failure is always there.

"The key difference between reengineering and other management techniques such as TQM, is that it is a frank acknowledgment that you are undertaking to radically change something, and that radical change is wanted and expected and necessary," he said.

"But, it is so big and affects so many areas, virtually no aspect of the organization is untouched. There are lots of opportunities to fail. People feel threatened and may try to torpedo the project. You can take on a project that is entirely too ambitious and just fail because nobody could handle the magnitude. You could fail to support the project adequately from the executive staff level or fail to give it the resources necessary to be successful. There are lots and lots of reasons that can lead to failure, but they all have to do with the fact that reengineering is really, really hard," he concluded.

"We believe good advance planning, such as we're starting to put together, will reduce our risk of failure," he continued. "Obviously, the continued commitment of PTO to the reengineering program also will go a long way toward reducing risk."

As a government organization, PTO is not constrained by bottom-line profit requirements. Thus, the Business Council has the luxury of taking a longer view and spending a little more money without having to realize benefits immediately. However, unlike many government agencies, PTO receives no direct appropriations from taxes, but instead is supported entirely by fees charged. Thus, the primary beneficiaries of the new reengineered systems will be those companies and individuals who use its services.

Even without a short-term profit motive, PTO's approach to BPR seems to be working. "The agency is trying to do this right," Liddle commented. "We are viewed with interest by the Department of Commerce because we have taken what appears to be a sound approach. We certainly believe we can become an example of how to do reengineering in the federal government."

The potential rewards for reengineering are huge in any organization, but are especially so in the federal government with hundreds of millions of taxpayer dollars at stake.

*A
Case Study
by
John McCloud*

Schlage Lock Co.

In 1991, as part of an on-going performance-improvement effort, San Francisco, Calif.-based Schlage Lock Co. initiated a business reengineering program designed to make the company better able to meet the demands of a changing marketplace. In particular, Schlage, which is part of Ingersoll-Rand Worldwide, wanted to accommodate the needs of the high-volume "value" retailers, such as Kmart, Wal-Mart, Home Depot and Builders Square, that dominate the retail market.

The company defined its primary reengineering goals as increasing throughput and productivity, reducing operations costs and improving customer relations. Preceding the decision to undertake process reengineering, Schlage adopted a Strategic Business Plan founded upon the following two objectives:

> *Vision statement* — Schlage business processes will define world class order management and manufacturing systems that provide premier customer satisfaction and support the Schlage Vision.

> *Mission statement* — The Strategic Information Systems Plan (SISP) Team will lead Schlage in the development and implementation of superior order management and manufacturing processes, systems and technologies that will delight the customer and support Schlage's strategic goals.

The business plan entails accomplishing the following:
- a 40 percent annual growth rate through 1996;
- 100 percent accuracy of orders;
- 100 percent on-time delivery (which translates as 2 day delivery from stock, 5 day shipment for non-master key orders, and 6 week shipment for master key and special orders); and
- a 75 percent reduction in the new product development cycle times.

In order to meet these goals, the plan envisions a significant increase in the use of automation. Most important, it envisions implementation of a the SISP, with process reengineering identified as a pivotal endeavor necessary to make the SISP work and ultimately bring the business plan to fruition.

As interpreted by Schlage, process reengineering entails defining, understanding, simplifying and documenting business and manufacturing processes in order to make them candidates for automation or other change. Attempting such changes was expected to have a major impact on company culture, as it would involve alteration in day-to-day operations, introduction of multifunctional processes and emphasis on teamwork. While the company's TQM philosophy provided an attitudinal foundation for this plan, implementation of the SISP provided the operational foundation.

In addition to business process reengineering, Schlage undertook several more conventional changes. These changes, it was assumed, would not only pave the way for reengineering, they would on their own provide benefits to the company's operations. These changes encompassed focusing marketing, sales, operations and financial results on four separate business units (commercial, residential, retail and international); consolidating customer accounts; and initiating basic on-going efforts toward product rationalization.

Responding to consumer trends
As it has done throughout its history, Schlage makes conventional key and combination locks. Although the company has improved and adapted its product over time, it has chosen not to enter the electronic or computer-coded card market. While Schlage offers service directly to companies and builders that need locks for specific sites or projects, the primary customer base consists of retailers, especially locksmiths, hardware and home improvement stores and some general merchandisers.

The company has approximately 2,500 employees and maintains facilities in five locations: San Francisco, which has headquarters and some manufacturing operations; San Jose, Calif. and Tecate, Mexico, which have manufacturing operations; Security, Colo., which has manufacturing and distribution; and Lenexa, Kan., which has distribution only.

At the time the decision to undertake reengineering was made, Schlage was not in crisis. Despite the recession, it has continued to enjoy healthy profits. Although the decline in residential and commercial construction has cut into the direct service business, a concomitant jump in home remodeling and a general escalation in security concerns has helped maintain strong retail sales.

However, the company recognized that its position in the industry would likely slip over the coming decade if it did not take steps to alter its methods of operation. Part of the concern stems from major changes in the way retailers operate. With rents at a premium, retailers have greatly reduced their own storage space, relying on frequent shipments rather than on-site reserves to replenish empty shelves. Although the majority of retailers today are large national chains that maintain their own centralized warehouse and distribution points, the number of stores being serviced and the need for high-volume sales mean that these central warehouses also do not have room for long-term stockpiling. They too rely on rapid turnover.

This in turn pushes the need for stockpiling onto the shoulders of the manufacturers. In the past, this was not a problem. Traditionally, Schlage projected needs based on previous sales, then manufactured and warehoused its product lines to match those projections. Production schedules for most items were set independent of actual orders. Some items ended up gathering dust for long periods, while supplies of some others ran short, but in general the system worked.

Under this method of operation, however, problems arise when customer demands do not follow expectations, and more and more frequently customer demands do not follow expectations. Thanks to rapid-turnover selling along with computer tracking, retailers can now practice micro-marketing, attempting to respond to consumer trends with as little delay as possible. Unfortunately for manufacturers, this kind of micro-marketing means they are expected to respond with equal rapidity. Projections based on last year's sales are no longer adequate. Now production must be based on last month's or even last week's sales, and the time required to get a particular item into and through production must be very short.

Schlage recognized that speeding up its own response time would require profound changes in operations that included implementation of a much more sophisticated information system than the one currently in use, significantly greater use of automation in the manufacturing process, reorganization of its marketing, sales and administration processes and, in order to make the preceding changes possible, retraining employees and giving them more reason and opportunity to become involved in meeting company goals.

Developing the SISP

At the end of 1991 Schlage began formulation of the SISP. The motivation behind the effort was to take an in-depth look into the critical business processes and provide a systemic plan of continuous improvement based on TQM concepts. According to company documents, the SISP "aims to provide a 21st century road map that will guide the IS department to apply the latest technology to serve the customer better and to support the goals of the strategic business plan."

To help focus its goals and ascertain the best theoretical and practical tools to use, the company brought in a consulting team from Price Waterhouse. The consultants worked with Brent Elliott, a Schlage manager with a background in finance and accounting, who was chosen to head up the reengineering effort. The initial period, which lasted four to five months, included interviews with approximately 60 Schlage employees from the various facilities. Participants were asked to outline their responsibilities, talk about critical strategies they had developed to complete their tasks, and contribute ideas for improvements to the company's information systems.

Additionally, Elliott formed a ten-person cross-functional, multi-site team, working under his direction, to develop the information systems plan. The team consists of systems analysts from the following divisions and departments:

- Schlage Division Office (San Francisco)
  - Order Entry Process
  - Master Schedule Process
  - Finance Process

- San Francisco Bay Area Manufacturing
  - Manufacturing Engineering & Design Engineering Process
  - Shop Operations & Quality Assurance Process

- Security, Colo. Manufacturing
  - Manufacturing Engineering & Design Engineering Process
  - Shop Operations & Quality Assurance Process

- Tecate, Mexico Manufacturing
  - Manufacturing Engineering & Design Engineering Process
  - Shop Operations & Quality Assurance Process

Elliott also has two assistants, including industrial engineer Sheryl Pounds.

Schlage wanted to have as many of the team members as possible hired from within the company, and the final count tallied eight existing Schlage employees and two new hires. Members were nominated either by themselves or by co-workers or managers. Only when no employee demonstrated the appropriate technical proficiency in a specific area or where no qualified employee opted to participate did the company recruit from external sources. The team members were chosen based on three primary criteria:

- expertise in one of the ten targeted company functions;
- willingness and liberty to engage in regular weekend and overtime work; and
- willingness and liberty to travel to other Schlage facilities and spend significant amounts of time away from home.

Secondary criteria included demonstration of "an achievement orientation and other critical competencies together with a high level of personal and professional commitment," as well as perceived capacity to grasp complex new ideas and methodologies. In addition, says Pounds, the company "looked for people who we felt understood what was happening on the floor. We wanted people who already had the inclination to look at the broader picture."

The team, which was selected in mid 1992, reports to a five-person sponsor group comprised of the managers of the company's worldwide manufacturing and commercial business units, the company controller, and the human resources and TQM directors. The sponsor group has responsibility for interfacing between the team and senior management, which has ultimate responsibility for all actions.

SISP and process reeengineering

Although the initial SISP investigatory effort focused on the software programs then in use, the interviews and subsequent team discussions revealed deeper problems.

"We had a lot of custom (software) programs, in house," explains Elliott. "And what we came up with is [that] we could actually go in and implement new systems to basically automate our existing practices. But as we were looking at where we were going strategically, we felt that just automating our current practices wasn't going to be enough for the future. We had to do something a lot more dramatic than just automating our current processes. Especially from an information standpoint."

Consequently, process reengineering became the cornerstone of company change and of the SISP. It would first be applied to the information system framework and then to manufacturing.

The SISP team in conjunction with the three company sponsors developed a communications process reengineering program. The program entailed cataloguing and simplifying the company's communications process, then applying appropriate technology to facilitate information exchange.

Seven critical business processes were chosen for an in-depth analysis in relation to the company's communications procedures and systems. These included order entry, product costing, design for producibility, bill of materials, master scheduling, order management and business systems support. Once the analyses were complete, the SISP team created a framework for development and implementation of a new information system.

Emphasizing the customer

The SISP team and its sponsors committed the company to an IS strategy of providing centralized planning with local execution. The SISP finally devised by the team was designed to emphasize customer service and focuses on five key areas:

- process reengineering;
- application recommendations;
- technology recommendations;
- IS management recommendations; and
- implementation plan.

The plan includes communication goals, measurements and

performance guidelines, as well as a commitment to significant investment in training of all system users in order to achieve the necessary shift in company culture. It involves streamlining information processes in each of the critical business processes, then evaluating computer applications to determine which ones best support those processes. The keys to success would be incorporation of user-friendly reporting capabilities and greater reliance on on-line, end-user computing.

Among the team's findings as expressed in the SISP were that by using more packaged software and fewer software vendors, company systems would become much more integrated, creating an information systems environment that allows quicker and more comfortable access to those systems. A higher priority was given to outsourcing the application than developing it in-house. Through outsourcing, the team determined the company would be able to reduce the software implementation cycle time.

Several evaluative criteria were used in the selection of a basic communications platform and the various application packages. The criteria were:

- level of integration with current applications;
- amount of in-house customization required;
- amount of paperwork reduced;
- ease of use;
- level of training required; and
- provision of additional functionality.

Historically the computing environment at Schlage had been oriented toward batch processing (53 percent batch vs. 47 percent on-line), using a mainframe computer. As the company strives to achieve 100 percent customer service levels in delivery and accuracy of orders, the SISP recognized that the percentage of on-line processing would have to increase substantially in order to enable quick response to customer enquiries. The final goal of the SISP is selection of a platform that supports on-line processing 90 percent of the time. The platform, it was determined, would have to be based on what is commonly referred to as "client server architecture" using personal computers.

The SISP also recognized that selection of a technology platform would commit Schlage to a certain level of computer operations and path of migration for the next few years. Thus it emphasized selection of a computing platform that allowed the company to keep up with changing technology. And the platform had to meet the following internal criteria:

- cost effectiveness;
- provision of end-users with the latest tools and databases;
- empowerment of end-users through on-line capabilities; and
- availability of packaged software.

Eight platforms were identified as meeting the criteria, and the IBM AS/400 platform using UNIX was identified as the one most likely to meet the IS goals.

Besides the main computing platform, the SISP studied Local Area Networks and Wide Area Network technologies that would link the engineering and sales offices and manufacturing and warehousing facilities to improve communication and cycle times. Electronic Data Interchange was also seen as a crucial link to facilitate improved customer and vendor relationships, with all stand-alone PCs ultimately to be connected to a LAN, thereby allowing the end-user greater access to applications and data.

"It's really putting the application as well as the user tools in the hands of the users," Elliott explains. "They will be able to work on a real-time basis and derive the information they need to help them make decisions… versus [the situation] in today's environment, [where] there's a lot of reports… written by a select few individuals. [If] I need a new report now… I've got to go to MIS to get that information out of the system. Or I have to have MIS programmers do it. In the future, we're looking at the users actually being able to have those skills and tools available to them to… derive the information they need and the format they need it in. This particular architecture helps in that process."

To assist with the selection and implementation stages, Schlage brought in a couple of computer consultants on a part-time basis. The consultants provided information on the kinds of hardware and software available, coached team members on technology applications and use and helped evaluate specific systems and programs.

As part of the commitment to maintaining quality over time, the SISP will be updated on an annual basis to reflect changes to Schlage's Strategic Business Plan and the progress of in-process projects.

Reengineering beyond the SISP

With the SISP completed and the communications technological platform selected, the company began simultaneous efforts to reorganize the manufacturing process based on implementation of the new information system. The foundation of the change in manufacturing was reorganizing from a line-work to a production cell orientation and retraining employees.

Schlage's traditional manufacturing pattern assigned a single task to each employee, who would perform that task and that task only. The approach created many inefficiencies. In particular, it often left some employees idle while backlogging work for others.

"Different tasks take different amounts of time," says Pounds. "Say in production a lock moves from station 7 to station 1. Station 7 can complete its work on 100 locks an hour, while station 1 can do 1,000 locks an hour. Station 1 ends up finishing all the work passed to it from station 7 in 10 minutes or so, then has to wait 50 minutes until another batch comes in."

Because the business consistently earned solid profits, these kinds of inefficiencies generally were ignored. However, under pressure of increased competition, the company recognized the necessity of reexamining these inefficiencies, looking at them both as an obstacle to meeting the current goals of the business plan and as an opportunity to push production beyond the targeted goals.

Working from ideas developed by Michael Hammer in *Reengineering the Corporation,* Schlage decided to divide its workforce into a series of cells, each of which would have responsibility for a particular group of product lines. Members of each cell would learn multiple tasks so that personnel could be shifted as labor needs changed with each step along the production process.

Members would also have a greater understanding of the entire process from concept to production through marketing and sales. They would know how their role, or rather roles, fit into the overall process, and they would be positioned to take a more proprietary interest in the product. Rather than facing a sometimes intermittent but nonetheless unending routine that as far as most individual workers could tell had no beginning and no end, they would be part of a team with clearly defined projects, explicit schedules and comprehensible goals.

To accomplish the reengineering, Schlage created a team for each of the company's five facilities. Claudia Melteff, the company's director of human resources, refers to this group as a "Tiger Team."

"It's an Army term," she explains. "The idea is it's a group that goes in and blitzes an area. We pulled together the brightest and the best and let them have a go at reorganizing."

Each facility has a "champion" whose has responsibility for making sure that resources are obtained and time schedules are adhered to. The champions, under Elliott's supervision, are accountable for implementing the new effort, for making sure company objectives are met as Schlage establishes goals for each reengineering process undertaken.

Elliott emphasizes that not all areas are amenable to reengineering. The time involved in reorganization would not produce sufficient savings or advantages to make it worthwhile. He points to maintenance as one such area.

"There's certain areas that we can get obviously much more results from than we can by reengineering everything," he notes. "Unless something is going to impact the process all the way along, it's probably not worth doing, at least at present." Once critical areas are reengineered, maintenance and other low-impact areas may become reasonable candidates for future efforts, Elliott adds.

Most of the changes at Schlage are in progress. The company has nearly completed the "migration" off its mainframe, but Elliott says certain tasks cannot be shifted until all others are in place and refined on the new system. Also, the company continues to modify its business goals, fine tuning target figures, eliminating duplication and adding additional objectives. For example, one new goal is to eliminate or reduce all nonvalue-added activities.

"When you look at... a manufacturing company, it's not uncommon to have only two and three percent of the total time it takes to fulfill an order be value-added, and the rest of it is nonvalue-added. It's the waiting. A rule of thumb that we're using is 10 percent value-added is world class within a manufacturing environment. Some of our processes come close to that; in other cases our processes exceed that. But overall, we're definitely much less than 10 percent, so that's what we're looking at, increasing the value of our total process...

"This may mean, you can be much more responsive given the same number of people, or you may find that you can put your resources to work in other areas that will actually add more value... We're very committed in training our associates so they can in the future even add more value, like coming up with new ideas or getting trained in areas that we're not necessarily doing a lot in at present."

The heaviest focus at present is determining the best measures to use in planning the reengineering of the various individual processes that make up Schlage's operation. The most pressing task in this regard is determining the exact requirements of the marketplace in terms of turnaround time. Elliott gives the example of the current 10-day cycle from the time manufacturing receives some orders to the time they are shipped out.

"If the marketplace tell us, 'I really need that particular product in three working days instead of 10', one of the objectives we would lay out is [getting that product out in] three days. So we're getting input from what our customers are really asking for and using that as our goal and target."

To accomplish that type of reduction, however, the company realizes that it will have to proceed in phases, first whittling down the cycle to perhaps seven days, then five and finally three.

"The objective is to make sure you envision where you want to go… but you may not be able to immediately get that just by saying… we're going to come in and have three days… The whole implementation process is a process to be managed," Elliott cautions.

He continues, "How do you first get all of the phases or the new process deployed? From the education of the people all the way through all the different processes to potentially changing the design of the manufacturing area — you may end up having to get benches in where you had an assembly line before, for example — how do you do that? The implementation process may be broken down in phases to get you down to the three days."

The reengineering effort at Schlage was undertaken in a top-down manner. Elliott, for example, reports to five executives on a direct line basis, including the three SISP sponsors. Although major goals include greater autonomy in the performance of individual jobs and the steps toward reaching that goal were developed by an employee-based team, the decision to introduce change was made at the executive level and the type of process chosen determined by senior management. Employees had no say in whether to undertake reengineering, nor in whether to participate or what areas would be candidates for change.

"If there's ideas that are generated at the lower levels to look at various processes, my bosses and I will evaluate those in the realm of priorities we have in front of us to determine what we need to do, whether we should entertain them or not," says Elliott. "But we have established a list of priorities that we need people to focus on and basically it's now a top down approach."

The impetus for change, according to Elliott, came from the appointment of Tom Field as president in 1990. Although the company had already begun looking into reengineering before Field came aboard, having someone at the top who was fervently committed to the approach appears to have played a central role in actually getting the program instituted.

"He's the one who's really initiated and helped drive some of the decision making down to lower levels, especially participation in decisions," says Elliott. "He's done a lot in getting other people involved in helping us strategically plan for the future. His basic management styles and philosophies are really getting us focused on changing the way we do business and driving us toward the future. He basically reinforced and preached the empowerment process and pushing accountability down, getting the input of other people before decisions are finalized and making sure we're making the right decisions."

Adds Pounds, "Reengineering has to start at the top if it's going to make very dramatic improvements. Even though that seems backwards [in terms of employee empowerment], it's only at the top level that you get the full view. People on the floor might have good ideas about how to improve the situation at their station or at the stations around them, but they can't see how it fits into the big picture, especially when they're spread out over five cities."

If there was a serious shortcoming to Schlage's approach, says Melteff, it occurred at the mid-management level. The traditional company culture focused on management development, with employees able to move up the ladder a step at the time. Advancement was accomplished via a combination of on-the-job experience and outside education. The company had a tuition reimbursement program for employees but offered no in-house training beyond the incidental learning that occurs through job performance.

The shift to a cellular structure, however, stood to eliminate or revise mid-management positions. Because of this, the company made what Melteff says was the mistake of skipping over mid-level managers when it began introducing new training programs as part of reengineering. Because mid-level managers had advanced through the ranks and consequently had the respect of other employees, who looked on them as professional models they could pattern their own careers after, failure to include them in the reorganization effort created distrust and in some cases hostility to change.

"We were managing this change as though this company was just a bunch of building blocks rather than people," says Melteff. "Although it's necessary to take risks, how do you make it comfortable for managers? We were giving the associates on the floor new skills, making their jobs more interesting and exciting, but we overlooked the people who were in supervisory positions. They ended up feeling superfluous."

This was not intended, says Melteff, since a primary objective throughout the reengineering effort was to preserve jobs. Downsizing was not an aim. Rather Schlage wanted to make more efficient use of existing employees. While the company anticipated changes in job description and some shifting of employees from one area to another, few layoffs were foreseen.

In fact, the company so far has lost only seven or eight positions total, with minimal employee turnover — except in Tecate, where, says Elliott, 10 percent to 15 percent turnover on a regular basis is not unusual. Nonetheless, says Melteff, the company's approach created more doubt than it need have.

"We were naive," she says. "We thought what we were doing would automatically improve communications, but I'm not sure everybody understood what we were doing. Reengineering was not positioned as an integral activity but as something that was being imposed."

Pounds stresses that good communication from the company and from team leaders is crucial since the reengineering process relies in turn on getting good communication back from workers.

"One of the hardest jobs is figuring out how do you pull information out of people who may not have thought about their jobs before. Most people don't spend time analyzing what they do. They just learn the job and do it. Now you have to find a way to get them to think about it and to persuade them that thinking about it is going to help them and help the company," she says.

Melteff believes the company's single greatest mistake was in not recognizing that people have an emotional attachment to their jobs, including to the way that job is done. A change in procedure is easily perceived as a threat.

"We fell down on communications," says Melteff. "We did a lot of ad hoc communication. We relied on the grapevine when we should have had a more strategic game plan. We had a lot of meetings and sent out a lot of letters, but we didn't plan a specific education and information campaign."

By not making it clear from the beginning that Schlage intended to preserve the majority of its positions and that it was not possible to know exactly which positions might end up being cut, Melteff says the company made it seem as if it might be hiding its motives when it wasn't. The shift from a hierarchical to cellular structure only added to the uncertainty.

"People like to see where they stand in an organization, but with reengineering, the lines of command aren't as clear anymore. In the end, I think most of the employees like the reorganization, but initially it can be frightening to lose the security that comes from a well-defined job," Melteff notes.

"We thought we could prevail by addressing everything with logic, but if you can't manage the feelings, that's where problems occur," she continues. "People aren't dumb. When a shake-up of any kind occurs, they know it's going to affect them, and their first reaction is going to be emotional."

The irony, Melteff points out, is that companies want people who are emotionally connected to their work. "That's where the commitment comes from. You want them to care."

Underlying the communications problems, says Melteff, was the decision not to assign a single top executive to oversee the entire reengineering effort. By having five people in line above Elliott, she says, the company opened the door for misunderstanding. With one person having final oversight, communication can be better coordinated and there is less risk of mixed, or missed, signals.

Despite these shortcomings, Elliott and Melteff believe Schlage's basic approach to reengineering is nonetheless more humane and effective than that of many other companies. In particular, Elliott mentions the decision to develop most measurements through the reengineering process rather than adopting them at the start as more responsive both to the market and to employee concerns.

He also trumpets the decision to use in-house teams rather than outside consultants. Although, from time to time Elliott does use an outside consultant to advise him from a more "global" viewpoint and to help him get a broader view on strategic issues and obstacles to change, he is adamant in his insistence that only company employees should be involved in working out the actual process.

"We don't use consultants within our reengineering efforts," he says. "We really believe that we have to do this ourselves. Each one of my people that I have reporting to me is extremely well trained in process reengineering techniques. So they're very much aware, and for the past year, each of them has been doing some degree of process reengineering within the company. [They know] what the issues are and what to look out for and what to be aware of as we do these process reengineering efforts."

A
Case Study
by
Susan Taylor

The Medical Center

As measured by operating costs, The Medical Center (TMC) in Beaver, Pa., is the most efficient hospital in western Pennsylvania. It also has excellent clinical quality and award-winning service departments. Yet, Bob Gibson, president and CEO of the hospital, believes there is a basic flaw in how hospitals deliver their services, and nothing short of a radical transformation of the whole organization will correct that flaw.

Using efforts in the manufacturing sector as a guide, Gibson is leading The Medical Center in a fast-track business process reengineering (BPR) strategy that eventually will compass every area of the hospital to achieve significant improvements in overall productivity and efficiency. The result will be a new, highly efficient organization built specifically around meeting patients' needs in terms of quality and service.

Customer friendly healthcare

TMC is a 470-bed non-profit hospital located about 35 miles northwest of Pittsburgh. It is the dominant healthcare provider in its service area and also is the area's largest single employer, with about 2,000 employees.

Beaver County is an area especially hard hit by the steel industry recession. Faced with local economic pressures and significant changes in government healthcare policies, hospital management went through a visioning process in 1990 to redefine TMC's mission. Maintaining market share continues to be a goal, but the mission has been broadened to take on the specific responsibility for improving the health of area residents. The vision contains a commitment to provide excellent healthcare at controlled costs, and it defines the specific quality, efficiency and customer satisfaction outcomes by which success will be measured.

"The visioning was difficult, but it clearly defined what we wanted to do, which was transform the organization," explained Kathy Adelman, vice president of corporate services. "We wanted to make the organization much more customer sensitive, much more responsive and more flexible. Moving from a product focus to a customer/patient focus was fundamental to the success of the new mission."

The management group also wanted to take a proactive approach to the inevitable reforms facing the entire healthcare industry. Expected changes in the healthcare reimbursement system, in particular, would require much greater levels of efficiency.

"Nobody knows what's going to happen with the national healthcare system, but whatever it is will move in the direction of rewarding efficiency and low cost," said Gibson. "Anything we do that makes us more efficient and lowers our cost has to put us in a better position. What the manufacturing industry calls reduced cycle time, we call reducing the length of stay. It's absolutely critical to our economic well-being."

"At the same time, I think there's an absolute correlation between customer satisfaction and efficiency. If we can cut the time it takes for a patient to get a pain pill from 2.5 hours to 18 minutes, it increases patient satisfaction and makes us more cost efficient," he continued.

As the hospital began focusing more on customers and improved service delivery, it became apparent that the hospital systems were, in fact, impeding many of its services.

"We knew we had a problem," Gibson said. "We worked hard to teach our people to be customer friendly, but it doesn't do any good to have customer friendly people if you still have to wait six hours in the Emergency Room, or if you get somebody else's meal tray, or they send you to radiology and lose you. It takes more than customer friendly people; the whole system has to be customer friendly."

The hospital began implementing Continuous Quality Improvement (CQI) techniques to improve its systems, but quickly found these efforts did not address the fundamental problems. "We concluded that all these CQI teams were making nice little changes, but there was something fundamentally wrong with the underlying structure. We were never going to solve the problem with CQI scratching the surface," Gibson explained.

Research into various quality initiatives led the hospital to Patient Focused Care. Because customer service is a key component of the hospital's new vision and values, Patient Focused Care sounded like a good solution.

Decentralizing around patient needs

Patient Focused Care (PFC) is an adaptation of the concept of work cells in manufacturing. It involves grouping patients with similar care and resource needs and then building necessary services around them.

For example, at TMC, orthopedics and neurology patients are grouped because they have many needs in common, including physical therapy, similar types of X-rays and similar blood work. The former Intensive Care Unit and Coronary Care Unit also are now combined into a Critical Care Patient Center because of similar patient needs. Decentralized versions of services such as labs, radiology, physical therapy and pharmacies are located right in the new patient centers. By 1995, TMC plans to have nine patient centers, each focusing on specific types of care.

"Before PFC, our industrial engineering studies showed that a normal patient in an average six-day stay traveled almost two miles in the hospital to get various tests, and spent hours on end waiting for various reasons (see figure 1). Also, patients were seeing as many as 70 different people during a hospital stay," explained Terry Biss, senior vice president.

With the new team-based approach, patients interact with fewer healthcare professionals and receive more personalized attention. All patient center staff are cross-trained to perform many job functions, effectively eliminating single-skill job functions. For example, personnel on the unit are cross-trained to draw blood for tests, which eliminates the need to have a person whose only job is drawing blood. In addition, services have been reorganized to provide for 80 percent of the resources right on the units. The new design will eliminate long waits, and will greatly reduce the need for patients to travel around the hospital to receive testing and other services.

Although the initial capital outlay is greater for decentralized services, the payback in terms of efficiency and patient satisfaction are tremendous. Decentralization is proving to be better for the patient, better for the nurses and physicians, and better for the hospital.

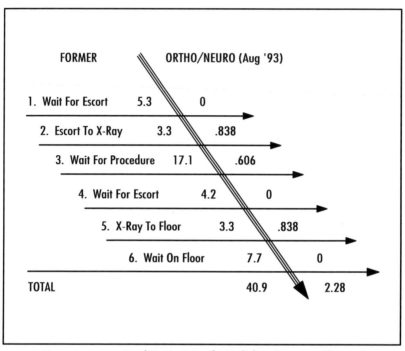

Figure 1. Average Total Waiting Time for Radiology Inpatients (Minutes)

Patients spend less time waiting. Nurses spend more time with hands-on care and less time with paperwork and non-value added activities. Lab or X-ray results can be provided to doctors within minutes, rather than the next day. Preliminary results of the patient units already operating show a measurable drop in average length of stay, and studies project that PFC will save the hospital several million annually in operating costs.

Change management perspective
After a year of intense effort to implement PFC, hospital management realized that while PFC is very effective, it really only affects about half the hospital. "The cold reality was that all the other support departments of the hospital were being pulled in several directions," Biss explained. "For the patient centers, they were being asked to decentralize and put all services on the units; but the needs of the rest of the hospital and the out-patients were not being addressed."

"We were re-designing our patient units and attempting to have them operate effectively within the existing system. It just didn't work," added Adelman. "From a change management perspective, we had not created a process or mechanism for the rest of the organizational structure to determine how best to serve the new patient units, as well as their other internal customers and the external customers — the outpatients.

"We realized that change goes beyond just the redesign of a physical plant. It gets into human development change, cross training, re-definition of jobs, changing information systems and changing management systems to support this new world," she continued.

At the same time, the design teams for the new patient centers were reaching the same conclusion. These teams, which include hourly employees, department directors and physicians, as well as architects and design engineers, realized very early in their planning that the whole institution would have to be changed. Rather than address this magnitude of change immediately, they chose to focus on getting all the PFC units operating first.

"When we brought up the first unit, we knew some things still needed changing on the centralized side," explained Joni Meiter, who heads the Critical Care Patient Center. "But once it was operating, the gaps became larger, not only in processes, but in staff. Some staff work part-time in the unit and part-time in the centralized department. It is like working in two different worlds, one with staff being empowered and headed toward self-directed work teams and one still very much manager directed."

On the process side, the biggest issue is scheduling patients back to the central departments when necessary. "In Critical Care, for example, it's very hard to move our patients. Although not all machines can be moved, we need a way to coordinate more around the patient rather than the service," Meiter added.

By late 1992, it was abundantly obvious that the hospital could not continue running dual systems. "When we are finished with PFC in 1995, we will have drastically changed the whole face of the hospital," Biss said. "We needed to sit down and think about all the processes in the hospital and how they would support that changed environment. That's when we took a broader scope approach and began looking into BPR."

Adelman convened a meeting of all middle managers and department heads and asked them to start thinking about alternative structures and how their departments could best meet the hospital's vision.

"From a change management perspective, it would have been better if we had made the vision operational for everybody up front, but we didn't," she commented. "As it turned out, the route we took is working, and I think it will continue to crystallize through the reengineering process."

The initial response from these department heads was mixed, however. Some were excited about the possibilities. Others were determined it would never work. Still others recognized the need for changes, but were unsure how to effect those changes. At the time, the hospital did not have a formal BPR plan or templates to show them. In retrospect, Adelman believes that probably was good.

"They needed time to think about it, get the seed planted, and resist some — because at the end they will feel more a part of it," she said. "At one of the later meetings, after they had established goals and determined what the organizational transformation meant to them, finally somebody raised his hand and asked for a template. By then, we had one to give him."

Pulling expertise from manufacturing sector

When BPR was identified as a strategic direction for the hospital, management understood it would be a long-term process, not a quick-fix project. Outside consultants were used for advice and facilitation, but an in-house champion and expert was needed to design and implement the formal BPR plan. The hospital maintains a small management engineering staff; however specific knowledge and experience in BPR was lacking.

In the search for a BPR project leader, Gibson never considered looking within the hospital industry. "Reengineering is not a prevalent course of action in hospitals. Plus, the whole idea of reengineering is to try to break through our healthcare paradigms. It didn't make sense to bring in a hospital person," he explained.

"From everything we could determine, very few within the hospital industry were doing anything novel to deliver services differently," Biss added. "Several hospitals were going through PFC, but that was all. However, manufacturing in the U.S., after going through drastic downsizing, had basically leaped the chasm and done some things that resulted in significant productivity gains, capital gains and WIP inventory reductions. We felt these techniques could be modified and applied up front to keep us from going through similar downsizing pains."

In June 1993, Patricia Kelly Lee, an industrial engineer with more than 11 years experience in manufacturing and consulting, was hired as reengineering project leader. Lee's assignment was to put together a fast-track BPR strategic plan with two main objectives. The short-term objective was to support the transition to PFC. The long-term goal was to develop an organizational structure that would support the hospital's vision for internal and external customers.

Structured to support and manage change

Top management leadership is critical to the success of any BPR project. At TMC, this leadership comes from an executive steering committee. Gibson's role on the committee is especially important and shows why he has chosen to continue as chief operating officer as well as CEO.

"I am THE driving force behind the vision," he said. "My job is to make it come alive, to free up and support those people who want to do a better job and somehow neutralize the people who want to slow everything down. To do that, I have to be right in there, in all the meetings, getting my hands dirty with everybody else."

Two basic service groups within the hospital, clinical/diagnostic and ancillary support services, are most affected by the changes already underway at the hospital, and therefore will be the focus of the first BPR projects. Future projects will focus on administrative services and financial systems, as well as external services such as home healthcare and outpatient clinics.

The clinical/diagnostic group includes radiology, laboratory, pharmacy, admissions, outpatient services, nuclear medicine and other special services such as cardiac rehabilitation and stress testing. Ancillary support services include such things as maintenance/engineering, dietary (including the cafeteria), materials management (including purchasing, storeroom, sterile processing, distribution, print shop, communications, contract management and escort), security, and housekeeping/laundry. Department heads from each area were formed into two BPR project teams which worked in parallel.

In addition to the department representatives, the BPR project teams also included representatives from information systems (IS), the PFC design teams, and public affairs, as well as Lee and members of the management engineering group. IS must support the new vision at the end, as well as the projects as they are being implemented. PFC representatives on the team validate ideas and ensure that the redesigned services can be integrated into the new patient centers.

The role of public affairs is to advise the groups on when and how to communicate ideas and plans. "You don't want to cause worry or undue concerns, but at the same time you want to communicate enough so people know where the hospital is headed," explained Terry Capp, public affairs director.

As they worked to redesign their business processes, the two BPR teams reported regularly to the steering committee for guidance and to ensure that the plans being considered fit with the overall hospital vision. The steering committee also was responsible for identifying and resolving possible inter-departmental bottlenecks.

Communications must travel down, as well as up. Thus, the department heads were charged with keeping their staff informed and involved with the changes being considered.

"We want to use a participative approach to process redesign," Adelman said. "These are the people who see the problems and challenges daily. They must identify with and evaluate the plan. They know what's right with the existing system."

First evaluate, then redesign

Using a model provided by First Consulting Group, Lee put together a plan that includes three major phases: process evaluation, which involves a comprehensive study of existing processes and systems; process redesign, which includes four redesign workshops and two recommendations sessions; and implementation. Figure 2 is a Gantt chart of the project timeline.

Process evaluation — The two BPR project teams were formed and began meeting in August. At the first meetings, the BPR plan was presented, along with templates for gathering data. The groups also had to develop team charters and rules and identify team coordinators.

"The team coordinator is critical," Lee commented. "This person has to be viewed as a leader from within the group, a process owner who has their best interests at heart."

The clinical/diagnostic group selected Ted Caveglia, director of radiology, as team coordinator. Caveglia had strong leadership skills and also was known for an ability to think ahead and envision a changed future. The ancillary support group is represented by Dennis Grady, director of materials management. Although he was not an early supporter of BPR, he was well respected by his peers. The steering committee was able to convince him of the value and importance of BPR. Once sold, he proved to be a valuable asset for selling BPR to his team and directing them through this process.

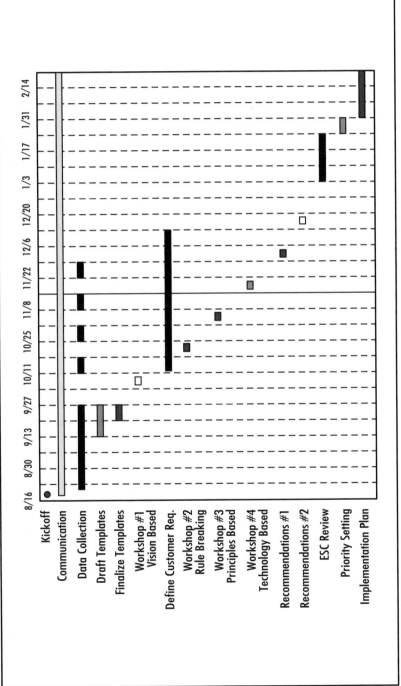

Figure 2. TMC's Reengineering of Clinical and Ancillary Services

During the evaluation phase, team members defined the specific processes and services each area provides to the organization, when and why they perform those services, the conditions under which they operate, and the specific output of those services. Each department identified its customers and the quality attributes they expected, as well as how actual performance ranked in terms of those attributes. They also discussed operating rules and assumptions, opportunities for improvement, and barriers to change. The actual written data collection was done over a five-week period by Lee and John Markowitz of the management engineering department, using templates provided by First Consulting.

A joint session of the two teams was held at the end of the process evaluation phase to improve understanding and transfer process knowledge among the departments about what each provides to the whole organization. At this meeting, department heads presented flowcharts showing what each department provides and how it interfaces with other departments, and discussed some possible opportunities for improvement.

Process redesign — The next step in TMC's BPR plan was to conduct the four redesign workshops with each team. At the time this case study was written, the first two workshops with each team had taken place. In the vision workshop, team members were asked to take the "clean sheet" approach and envision the perfect process without regard to current constraints and assumptions. The focus was on high level concepts, and major success factors were identified.

During the second workshop, the teams were asked to break the rules. Members identified current operating rules, both written and unwritten, and then evaluated their impact on cycle time, cost and service quality. The teams then came up with new rules for the process envisioned in the first workshop and evaluated them against the same process metrics of time, cost and quality.

BPR, as defined by Michael Hammer and successfully practiced by many companies, involves specific principles including the need to organize around outcomes instead of tasks, be flexible in anticipation of future needs, put decision points where work is performed, treat geographically dispersed resources as if they were local, build and enhance strategic links with other external and internal entities, and capture information once and only at the source. In the third workshop, TMC's BPR teams examined the idealized processes and rules established in the first two workshops to ensure that they incorporated these principles.

The final workshop was technology focused. At this point, the teams developed the requirements for the information systems and technology needed to support the reengineered business.

The timeframe for the four workshops was tight, with only two weeks between each workshop. The first two workshops were held in October, and the second two were held one month later. After each workshop, the reengineering project leader and the team coordinators attended a debriefing with the executive steering committee.

Following the last workshops, two recommendation sessions were held to formulate and then finalize plans. Plans for communicating the new redesign to employees, physicians and the public also were developed in these two sessions.

Overcoming resistance

As might be expected in any organization involved in BPR, not everyone at TMC was an enthusiastic supporter of reengineering at the beginning. Many feared the effort was just an excuse for downsizing.

"We had to convince them we didn't have a hidden agenda," said Lee. "We even took the step of changing some of the data gathering forms to eliminate any questions that might lead to concerns about job elimination."

"We countered some of that fear by convincing our employees that we are not a stationary hospital," added Biss. "We are constantly planning new programs and looking at ways to expand in the future. If PFC or reengineering does result in an opportunity to streamline certain operations, it will free up personnel to fill in some of these new positions in growth areas."

The hospital has a "no-layoff agreement" with its employees. Extensive company-paid re-training and cross-training programs ensure continued employment in new roles.

Resistance also came from those who believed their processes already were very efficient and did not need radical change. "One of our departments, housekeeping, has received national recognition for outstanding service. It is a challenge for them to understand what reengineering might mean to them," explained Capp.

This attitude was particularly obvious during the first set of workshops, in which teams were asked to envision the perfect process. The ancillary support team, in particular, resisted the "clean sheet" approach, and instead spent the time trying to build bridges between the way services are delivered now and the new patient centers.

The clinical/diagnostic team members, on the other hand,

were able to pull themselves out of their functional responsibilities and focus on similarities in how they accomplish services. One model they are considering involves shared pre-processing (i.e., patient registration and scheduling), a diagnostic services cluster, and a common post-processing area (i.e., report transcription and preparation, storage and retrieval processes, patient charging and checkout). They were able to describe the characteristics of the new process and develop a conceptual model for the future.

During the executive steering committee debriefing that followed the vision workshops, the ancillary support team coordinator realized his group had not fully accepted the goals and principles of BPR. Before the second workshop began, he solicited and received individual consensus and support from each team member to take a true clean sheet approach.

As a result, this group's second session went extremely well. "While the vision workshop was hard for them, they really knew their operating rules," commented Lee. "In fact, after grouping their operating rules, they could see more clearly how to envision the perfect process and which rules should apply in the new environment. It was easier for them to do the visioning and design in more manageable pieces."

After a good start, the clinical support group actually fell behind during the second workshop because team members got too caught up in the minutiae of the rules. "One of the risks of these workshops is that groups tend to get involved in too many details or in problem solving," Lee said. "Or else they constrain themselves by the limitations of the current systems. We (Lee, the management engineers, and an outside consultant from First Consulting) had to pull them out of that."

The team held an extra session between the scheduled workshops to catch up, and were back on track by the end of October.

Catching flaws before they are fatal

TMC has found that a good BPR plan must be flexible enough to incorporate additions and changes based on key learnings during the process. Several important changes have come out of the early workshops. One of the most important findings after the first workshop was the lack of customer feedback in the model being used. During the visioning process, team members realized their definition of the perfect process might not be the same as the customers'.

"With BPR, you should start with the customer and work

backward, instead of starting with your systems and working toward the customer," Lee explained. "Our original approach neglected that customer focus."

To correct that oversight, Lee formed a sub-group that included herself, the PFC transitional leader, the PFC project manager, three management engineers, the public affairs director, and a member of the marketing staff with expertise in customer surveys. This sub-group asked each department to identify primary and secondary customers of its services. Primary customers are being led through a visioning process similar to the workshop. Rather than register complaints about the current system, they are asked how services would be delivered in a perfect world. Written surveys are being sent to secondary customers.

Benchmarking is another area neglected by the original model. "We will have to benchmark, but certainly not with hospitals," Lee said. "We are considering many different industries. Federal Express may be a good benchmark for the transportation part of our services. Health spas are another consideration. We're trying to push our imagination to the limits in terms of benchmarking."

The early workshops also identified the need to have IS involved from the very beginning, rather than wait until the last workshop. "Although it wasn't part of our initial team structure, we now have Estelle Kemerer, IS director, involved in each workshop, as well as the debriefing sessions. She has been a tremendous benefit by reminding us not to get bogged down by the limitations of our current system, but instead to focus on the ideal design."

The teams also felt that while some services should be decentralized, others were best left centralized. However, they lacked guidelines for making that decision. Lee developed an algorithm with specific criteria for determining whether a service should be centralized or decentralized.

Implementing the reengineered processes
Preliminary ideas already are surfacing in the workshops. For example, one option would be to use the business unit concept to create a new clinical/diagnostic service cluster with shared business processes. Packaged services with one standard fee for each package also are being considered. A package, for example, might include one radiology test, one lab test including certain blood work, and some sort of EKG. Many of the ideas being considered come from the manufacturing industry, such as the use of shop routing and barcoding

techniques to move patients through the system more efficiently.

Although preliminary concepts are being discussed, the reengineering plan was not finalized until the steering committee approved it. The steering committee identified the costs, resources, and impact on the organization associated with each model, and also considered prioritized need and timing of implementation before choosing final BPR plans. Once models were finalized, the BPR project teams developed the transitional plan and then implemented the reengineered processes immediately. Full implementation is expected to take about two years.

Outside consultants are being used to facilitate workshops and provide templates and methodology, but their involvement in the implementation process will be limited. "Hospital staff are taking on the responsibility for the redesign and the implementation. We will be held accountable for making it fly," said Lee.

During the implementation phase, the steering committee will continue to manage the project. "Our criteria and measures during implementation will be things like clinical quality, customer satisfaction (both external and internal), efficiency and employee satisfaction," explained Adelman.

She emphasized that clinical quality is the most important of these criteria. The hospital is using critical path development to define quality in terms of specific outcomes. "Clinical quality clearly defines how support services need to function and operate for the clinical outcomes we're trying to produce," she said.

Achieving the vision throughout the organization
TMC is spending millions of dollars and an enormous amount of effort to transform every aspect of the hospital. While big bucks and hard work do not guarantee success, Gibson has not even considered the possibility of failure. He believes the keys to success are intense focus on the hospital vision and values, a careful coordination of reengineering with other management concepts, and healthy doses of blind faith and stubbornness.

"The pressure to slow down is overwhelming," he said. "My role, more than anything else, is to work around those people who keep telling me there is too much unrest. Even the consultants are telling us we're trying to go too fast and do too much. I'm just ignoring all of that and going full speed ahead. If I don't do that, I think we will fail."

Gibson also firmly believes that reengineering is not a stand-alone concept. "A whole set of things must come together to make for a successful rebirth of a company," he said. "All the culture changes, retraining managers to be leaders, cross training of job functions, empowering workers and self-directed work teams — it sounds like a string of cliches, but I really believe in that stuff. It's not just theory.

"An old Chinese proverb says 'You can't leap a chasm in two bounds,'" he continued. "A lot of people try to do that, and they never see their efforts as an integrated whole. Most people fail because they somehow don't understand how it all fits together."

Adelman added that many companies adopt CQI, reengineering, or whatever the latest management concept is, figure out how to put it into the organization, and never think about how it all relates in terms of the company's overall mission, vision and basic business. "If you put CQI, clinical quality and PFC on separate paths, you are doomed to fail, because the outcome depends on how they work together," she said.

To counter that problem, the executive steering committee at TMC has taken on the task of ensuring that all these efforts dovetail to achieve the ultimate vision and objectives. For example, once the hospital is redesigned, standard CQI concepts will be one of the foundations that ensure efforts keep moving in the right direction.

"We are spending a lot of time defining and redefining what these concepts mean to us and how a project fits into the whole," Adelman continued.

Gibson is convinced that achieving the hospital vision is not only best for the healthcare of Beaver County residents, but also is the only way the hospital will survive and grow in the future. "In some form or another, healthcare reform is coming. I have to believe that if we design the system to be more efficient, we're doing the right thing. Costs will go down and productivity will improve."

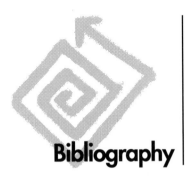

Bibliography

Carr, David C. et al. 1992. *Breakpoint Business Process Redesign.* Arlington, Va.: Coopers & Lybrand.

Crego, Edwin T., Jr. and Peter D. Schiffrin. 1994. *Customer Centered Reengineering.* Burr Ridge, Ill.: Irwin Professional Publishing.

Dichter, Steven F. 1991. The organization of the '90s. *The McKinsey Quarterly, #1*: 145-155.

Drucker, P.F. 1988. The coming of the new organization. *Harvard Business Review.* January-February 45-53.

Errico, Stephen G. and Anthony D. Sullivan. 1983. Radical is change: can we get there from here? *CASE News.* March: 16-19.

Hammer, Michael and James Champy. 1993. *Reengineering the Corporation: A Manifesto for Business Revolution.* New York, N.Y.: HarperCollins.

Harbour, Jerry L. 1994. *The Process Reengineering Workbook: Practical Steps to Working Faster and Smarter Through Process Improvement.* White Plains, N.Y.: Quality Resources.

Institute of Industrial Engineers. 1993. *Business Process Reengineering: Current Issues and Applications.* Norcross Ga.: Industrial Engineering and Management Press.

Johansson, Henry J. et al. 1993. *Business Process Reengineering: Breakpoint*

Strategies for Market Dominance. New York, N.Y.: John Wiley & Sons.

Kaplan, Robert G. and Laura Murdock. 1991. Core process redesign. *The McKinsey Quarterly, #2:* 27-43.

Leibfried, Kathleen H.J. and C.J. McNair. 1992. *Benchmarking: A Tool for Continuous Improvement.* New York, N.Y.: HarperCollins.

Lowenthal, Jeffrey N. 1994. *Reengineering the Organization: A Step-by-Step Approach to Corporate Revitalization.* Milwaukee, Wis.: ASQC Quality Press.

Martin, James A. 1990. *Information Engineering: Book II – Planning and Analysis.* Englewood Cliffs, N.J.: Prentice-Hall.

McDermott, Robin E., Mikulak, Raymond J., and Michael R. Beauregard. 1993. *Employee Driven Quality: Releasing the Creative Spirit of Your Organization Through Suggestion Systems.* White Plains, N.Y.: Quality Resources.

Monden. Y. 1993. *Toyota Production System, Second Edition.* Norcross, Ga.: Industrial Engineering and Management Press.

Moore, John. 1992. Reengineering riddle. *Systems and Network Integration.* May 18: 38.

Morris, Daniel and Joel Brandon. 1993. *Reengineering Your Business.* New York, N.Y.: McGraw-Hill.

Parry, Scott B. 1994. *From Managing to Empowering: An Action Guide to Developing Winning Facilitation Skills.* White Plains, N.Y.: Quality Resources.

Petrozzo, Daniel and John C. Stepper. 1994. *Successful Reengineering: An Indepth Guide To Using Information Technology.* New York, N.Y.: Van Nostrand Reinhold

Roberts, Lon. 1994. *Process Reengineering: The Key to Achieving Breakthrough Success.* Milwaukee, Wis.: ASQC Quality Press.

Schneider, William E. 1994. *The Reengineering Alternative: A Plan For Making Your Current Culture Work.* Burr Ridge, Ill.: Irwin Professional Publishing.

Scott Morton, Michael S. 1991. *The Corporation of the 1990s: Information Technology and Organizational Transformation.* Oxford, U.K.: Oxford University Press.

Shores, A. Richard. 1994. *Reengineering the Factory: A Primer for World-Class Manufacturing.* Milwaukee, Wis.: ASQC Quality Press.

Spechler, Jay. 1993. *Managing Quality in America's Most Admired Companies.* Norcross, Ga.: Industrial Engineering and Management Press.

Tichy, N.M. 1983. *Managing Strategic Change.* New York, N.Y.: John Wiley & Sons.

Tsang, E. 1993. Business process re-engineering and why it requires business event analysis. *CASE News.* March: 8-15.

Index